Series / Number 07-078

D0921388

DATA THEORY AND DIMENSIONAL ANALYSIS

WILLIAM G. JACOBY
University of South Carolina

SAGE PUBLICATIONS
The International Professional Publishers
Newbury Park   London   New Delhi

For information address:

SAGE Publications, Inc.
2455 Teller Road
Newbury Park, California 91320

SAGE Publications Ltd.
6 Bonhill Street
London EC2A 4PU
United Kingdom

SAGE Publications India Pvt. Ltd.
M-32 Market
Greater Kailash I
New Delhi 110 048 India

H
61.27
.J3c
1991

Printed in the United States of America

International Standard Book Number 0-8039-4178-1

Library of Congress Catalog Card No. 91-0000

FIRST PRINTING, 1991

Sage Production Editor: Diane S. Foster

When citing a university paper, please use the proper form. Remember to cite the current Sage University Paper series title and include the paper number. One of the following formats can be adapted (depending on the style manual used):

(1) WELLER, S. C., & ROMNEY, A. K. (1990) Metric Scaling: Correspondence Analysis. Sage University Paper Series on Quantitative Applications in the Social Sciences, 07-075. Newbury Park, CA: Sage.

OR

(2) Weller, S. C., & Romney, A. K. (1990). *Metric scaling: Correspondence analysis* (Sage University Paper series on Quantitative Applications in the Social Sciences, series no. 07-075). Newbury Park, CA: Sage.

CONTENTS

SERIES EDITOR'S INTRODUCTION

How do mere *observations* become *data* for analysis? Suppose, for example, a survey researcher conducts interviews with 1000 American consumers. The raw observations (think of checkmarks on an interview schedule) must be identified, labeled, and coded before they become data. How the researcher moves from observations to data is an interpretive act, one that data theory seeks to explain. Clyde Coombs, the pioneer in this area, developed a geometric view. Imagine a pair of elements, for example, a student and an exam item. A pair of elements may be selected from the same set or different sets, and the relation between the elements may be one of dominance or proximity. With these two distinctions, Coombs managed to classify any observation into one of four data types: single stimulus, stimulus comparison, similarities, and preferential choice.

As Dr. Jacoby makes clear, an understanding of data type is important, for it directs the researcher to the preferred scaling technique. Most data are single stimulus, suggesting the use of summated rating scales, the cumulative model, or factor analysis. In contrast, stimulus comparison data suggest the use of paired comparisons or, perhaps, psychophysical magnitude scaling. With similaries data, multidimensional scaling is preferred. Finally, preferential choice data are usually analyzed with the unfolding model. Further, within each type, a grasp of data theory offers guidelines; for example, when a probabilistic cumulative scaling technique might be selected over Guttman scaling.

This monograph is especially valuable in that it offers a theoretical, as well as applied, integration of disparate scaling techniques that have been treated separately in earlier series monographs: *Multidimensional Scaling* (Kruskal and Wish, no. 11), *Introduction to Factor Analysis* and *Factor Analysis* (Kim and Mueller, nos. 13 and 14), *Unidimensional Scaling* (McIver and Carmines, no. 24), *Magnitude Scaling* (Lodge, no. 25), and *Three-Way Scaling and Clustering* (Arabie, Carroll, and DeSarbo, no. 65). Beyond this integrative role, Dr. Jacoby's work also helps break new ground by explicating Alternating Least Squares, Optimal Scaling (ALSOS). This approach, based on data theory notions, holds out promise for regression estimation in the face of ordinal independent variables. The ALSOS discussion underlines one of his key conclusions:

"Specific variable values . . . are never immutable characteristics of the observations."

—*Michael S. Lewis-Beck*
Series Editor

DATA THEORY AND DIMENSIONAL ANALYSIS

WILLIAM G. JACOBY
University of South Carolina

1. INTRODUCTION

This monograph examines some basic ideas of data theory, and considers their implications for research strategies in the social sciences. For many readers, the very idea of a data theory is probably unfamiliar. After all, data are used to *test* theories. They are usually taken as given, fixed quantities when they are used as the input for some statistical modeling technique. Data are not generally regarded as the subject matter of theory in and of themselves. Nevertheless, any empirical investigation rests upon assumptions about the meaning of the observations it employs. In most cases, these assumptions are taken for granted, and are left unstated. The usual understanding seems to be that empirical observations can only be interpreted in the manner specified by the researcher. But this is emphatically not the case: Any empirical observation can be used to generate several different kinds of data. Of course, the nature of the data that are selected by the researcher will have a profound impact on any subsequent analyses that he or she might perform. Given this, it is important to develop a general set of assumptions about the connections among empirical observations, data, and methods of analysis. These assumptions should be sufficiently general to be applicable to virtually any situation that a researcher might encounter. This is precisely what a theory of data tries to provide.

AUTHOR'S NOTE: *I would like to express my gratitude to Saundra K. Schneider. She provided an enormous amount of editorial advice, artistic talent, and moral support throughout this project. The monograph could not have been completed without her help. I would also like to thank Herbert Weisberg, Henry Heitowit, and Wijbrandt van Schuur for their suggestions and comments. Finally, a special thanks goes to George Rabinowitz. He gave me my first exposure to many of these ideas, and he has been a constant source of advice, encouragement, and assistance.*

3

Definition of Data Theory

Data theory examines how real world observations are transformed into something to be analyzed — that is, data. Any empirical observation provides the observer with information. Typically, however, only certain aspects of this information will be useful for analytic purposes. The researcher takes a vitally important step in his or her analysis simply by culling out those pieces of information that are used from those that could be considered, but are not. The information that is used comprises the data, and it is clearly only a subset of observable reality. Hence, it is important to distinguish between observations (the information that we can see in the real world around us) and data (the information that we choose to analyze). The central concern of data theory is to specify how the latter are derived from the former.

Objectives of This Monograph

The main goal of this monograph is to integrate the material from the other Sage University Papers on scaling techniques (e.g., *Multidimensional Scaling* by Kruskal and Wish, the two volumes on factor analysis by Kim and Mueller, *Unidimensional Scaling* by McIver and Carmines, and *Three-Way Scaling and Clustering* by Arabie, Carroll, and DeSarbo. The objective is to place the various scaling strategies within a general context, rather than leaving them as separate and unrelated ways of analyzing data. On a more practical level, this monograph will cover information that is not widely known or available in the social science community. In so doing, it should address the kinds of questions that arise as people first learn about scaling methods. This monograph introduces a perspective on data that is useful for both intrinsic reasons and for instrumental purposes. On the one hand, data theory helps researchers gain a greater understanding of the objects they examine, by systematically revealing the ways that the objects differ among themselves. On the other hand, data theory facilitates more effective utilization of scaling techniques. This leads to higher quality measurement, which, in turn, can be used to generate stronger conclusions from empirical analyses.

2. MEASUREMENT

Measurement is defined as the process of applying numbers to objects in meaningful ways (Stevens, 1951). Although this simple statement captures the essential meaning of measurement, it is useful to examine the process in somewhat greater detail. Measurement always begins by placing a set of empirical objects into mutually exclusive, exhaustive categories. This classification process is based upon some attribute of the objects. In other words, objects are placed in the same category if they are identical with respect to the attribute; objects in separate categories differ with respect to the attribute. This classification task becomes measurement when numbers are assigned to the categories (and by implication, to the objects within the categories). The numerical assignment must possess an important property: The differences between the numbers assigned to the objects must reflect, in some specified way, the differences between the objects with respect to the attribute.

Measurement as Theory Testing

From the preceding discussion, it is easy to see that measurement involves constructing a formal model of a data set. The components of the formal model consist of the real number set, along with some or all of the properties of real numbers. Measurement occurs when the researcher applies the abstract model (consisting of selected aspects of the real number system) to an attribute or property of a set of empirical objects. But models are, by definition, abstractions. They can represent reality with greater or lesser accuracy. If a model is to provide a close reflection of an empirical system, then its logical implications must be worked out and compared with the observable behavior of the empirical objects in question. If the empirical observations are consistent with the model-based predictions, then we can conclude that the model provides an acceptable description of that segment of reality. This process of comparing abstract models against the empirical world is the central focus of scientific theory construction (Kaplan, 1964). This leads to an extremely important conclusion: All measurement is theory testing, because it involves examining the goodness of fit between an abstract model and a property of a set of empirical objects (Coombs, Raiffa, and Thrall, 1954).[1]

Implications. The view that measurement is theory testing has several important consequences. The most important is that measurement is never immutable; it is always a tentative statement about the nature of reality. Like any other theory, measurement systems are falsifiable. Falsification occurs whenever the specified properties of the real number system do not correspond to the empirical property under investigation.[2] At the same time, measurement systems, like other theories, can never be proven true. Regardless of prior empirical support for any particular assignment of numbers to objects, there may be instances, as yet unobserved, where the system is inconsistent with the real-world phenomena. Thus any measurement system, no matter how routinely it is carried out, is potentially open to revision, because of the constant need for consistency between the abstract number system and the real world.

In practical situations, the degree to which researchers actually test their measurement theories is often quite limited. Data values are simply taken as given quantities. Nevertheless, it is more appropriate to view the results of *any* measurement operation as tentative and malleable, rather than as fixed properties. This perspective has direct consequences for testing *substantive* theories. Consider the following scenario: A researcher develops a model to account for some form of social behavior, and generates testable hypotheses that can be compared against empirical data. However, upon carrying out the tests, the model-based predictions are not supported. The usual conclusion drawn in this situation is that some aspect of the model is inappropriate. But from a broader perspective, it is important to remember that the data values used in the empirical tests are, themselves, a model of the original observations. The falsification of theoretical propositions could be attributable to problematic aspects of the measurement, as well as shortcomings in the substantive model (Blalock, 1982). Therefore, it is appropriate to examine the correspondence between the measured values and the observations, just as it is to evaluate relationships among measured variables. This idea is, perhaps, one of the most important recent innovations in social statistics. For example, covariance structure models (e.g., LISREL) explicitly analyze both the relationships among concepts, and the linkages from concepts to indicators. And the simultaneous analysis of measurement and statistical models is a central feature of the optimal scaling strategy for measurement, discussed below. In any event, a more flexible view of the measurement characteristics possessed by empirical variables can often lead to more effective exploitation of the information contained in a data set.

Levels of Measurement

Levels of measurement represent variations in the ways that numbers are applied to objects. Although there are potentially many different measurement levels, only a handful seem to receive much attention (Coombs, Raiffa, and Thrall, 1954). These are the four familiar levels identified by S. S. Stevens (1946) — nominal, ordinal, interval, and ratio.

Measurement Level as a Function. For present purposes, it is more useful to view measurement levels in terms of the function transforming empirical observations into numerical values (Young, 1981). We will denote this function as f. Assume that S is a set of objects (with elements S_1, S_2, etc.) that vary with respect to some attribute. As explained above, the objects in S are categorized with respect to this attribute. M is a set of real numbers, which are placed in a one-to-one relation with the elements of S so that $M(S_1)$ is the number assigned to S_1, whereas $M(S_2)$ is the number assigned to S_2, and so on. The function f maps the elements of S into M. The nature of f determines the level of measurement.[3]

At the nominal level, f simply preserves the identity of the categories. That is, all objects within a given category are assigned the same number, and those in different categories are given different numbers. Thus:

$$f^n: \quad (S_1 = S_2) \rightarrow M(S_1) = M(S_2) \qquad [2.1]$$

$$(S_1 \neq S_2) \rightarrow M(S_1) \neq M(S_2) \qquad [2.2]$$

Beyond these simple restrictions, f^n (the superscript n means "nominal") places no limitations on the way the numbers are assigned to the objects. Note that the "=" on the left-hand side of equations 2.1 and 2.2 does not indicate mathematical equality. Instead, this symbol only represents equivalence in terms of the measured attribute. Therefore, the relation $(S_1 = S_2)$ means that these two objects fall in the same category with respect to the attribute. But these two objects are not, in any numerical sense, "equal" to each other. On the other hand, the "=" on the right-hand side is mathematically meaningful, because we can compare the magnitudes of the two numbers $M(S_1)$ and $M(S_2)$ to each other.

At the ordinal level, we maintain the equality restrictions that were used at the nominal level. But we also impose an ordering restriction on the elements of M, so that the function for an ordinal measure is defined as follows:

$$f^o: \quad (S_1 = S_2) \rightarrow M(S_1) = M(S_2) \qquad\qquad [2.3]$$

$$\text{Either} \quad (S_1 < S_2) \rightarrow M(S_1) \leq M(S_2) \qquad\qquad [2.4]$$

$$\text{or} \quad (S_1 < S_2) \rightarrow M(S_1) \geq M(S_2) \qquad\qquad [2.5]$$

In this case, the transformation f^o (the superscript o means "ordinal") preserves empirical asymmetries among the observational categories. Note that equations 2.4 and 2.5 both fulfill this condition equally well. Therefore, the choice between them is entirely up to the researcher; as a result, the directionality of an ordinal variable is completely arbitrary. Once again, we must be extremely careful when interpreting the "<" on the left-hand side of equations 2.4 and 2.5. Here, it indicates some substantive asymmetry between S_1 and S_2. There does not need to be anything intrinsically quantitative about the relation between these objects. The quantification expressed by $M(S_1)$ and $M(S_2)$ is, again, a construction of the researcher. Of course, the inequality on the right-hand side does express a mathematical relation between two numbers, but it is simply a result of the way the analyst chooses to interpret the observation.

The interval and ratio levels can be treated together. Here, f must be a specific numeric function relating S to M. The simplest case would specify a linear function from the observations into the numeric values[4]

$$f^i: \quad M(S_1) = a + b\,(S_1) \qquad\qquad [2.6]$$

where a and b are real-valued coefficients. The ratio level of measurement is identical, with an additional requirement that:

$$f^r: \quad a = 0 \qquad\qquad [2.7]$$

This additional restriction reflects the fact that with ratio measurement, the location of the origin is substantively meaningful; that is, the zero value in the assigned numbers corresponds to some characteristic of the observations. Note that interval/ratio measurement typically requires more information about the underlying objects than is necessary at the other levels. The nominal and ordinal levels are formally defined by comparisons across objects. This is not the case for interval or ratio measures. Once values of a and b are specified, then each S_i can be assigned its proper $M(S_i)$ completely apart from any other observations. Of course, a researcher's willingness to specify any function of this kind depends entirely on his or her knowledge of the attribute under examination.

Indeterminacy of Measurement Values. An important consequence of the preceding approach to measurement levels is that *any* set of numbers satisfying f provides an equally good measure of the attribute under consideration. For example, assume that M_1 and M_2 are two entirely different sets of numbers for representing S. Further, assume nominal measurement, so that the conditions in equations 2.1 and 2.2 hold true. In this case, M_1 and M_2 are functionally equivalent measures of S. There is no mathematical or logical reason inherent in the measurement process for choosing M_1 over M_2 or vice versa. Similarly, any measures M_1, M_2, and so on, that satisfy equations 2.3 and 2.4 (or 2.5) provide identically appropriate ordinal measurement, and so on. Looking at the problem this way emphasizes that there is no single "correct" measurement for any attribute. It is always possible to find another set of numbers that represents the objects equally well.

As we have just seen, there are an infinite number of possible measures for any variable, regardless of the measurement level. But it is true that the nature of f becomes more restrictive as we move from the nominal level up through the ratio level. This is illustrated graphically in Figures 2.1 through 2.4. In each panel of the figure, the horizontal axis represents the empirical objects. Locations along this axis correspond to distinct categories of the attribute under observation. At the nominal level, the ordering of the categories is arbitrary. For the other three measurement levels, assume that the categories are arrayed in some substantively meaningful way. The vertical axis in each panel represents the numbers assigned to the objects. In Figure 2.1, the circular points graph a function that might be associated with a nominal variable. But any other set of plotted points (such as the triangular points) would be an equally accurate graph of this variable, so long as no two points with distinct coordinates on the horizontal axis are given the same coordinates on the vertical axis, and vice versa. Obviously, this imposes very few limitations on the transformation from objects to numbers. The solid line in Figure 2.2 shows a function for an ordinal variable. The graph reflects the asymmetry of the empirical objects: Moving from left to right on the horizontal axis, the numerical values never decrease. But again, this condition is not very restrictive; any other monotonic plot (such as either of the dotted lines in the figure) would provide an equally accurate depiction of the objects. Figure 2.3 shows an interval variable. Here, any one of the plots is just as

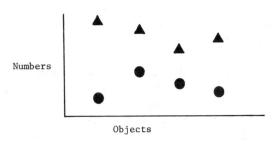

Figure 2.1. Graph of Functions for Nominal Level Measurement

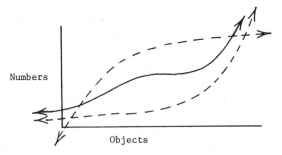

Figure 2.2. Graph of Functions for Ordinal Level Measurement

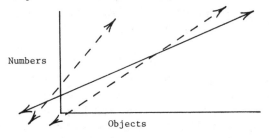

Figure 2.3. Graph of Functions for Interval Level Measurement

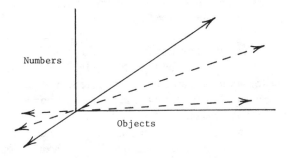

Figure 2.4. Graph of Functions for Ratio Level Measurement

good as any other in the graph. However, the function is always linear; it is just that the values of *a* and *b* that are completely arbitrary. Figure 2.4, showing a ratio level variable, is even more restrictive. Although any slope is permissible (and, from a strict measurement perspective, fully equivalent), the intercept is fixed at zero. Thus the nature of the measurement function becomes increasingly restrictive as we move from the nominal to the ratio levels. Still, this leaves an infinite number of possible measures for each of the levels.[5]

Given the enormous latitude in assigning numbers, how does a researcher choose between the various permissible measures, M_i, for a particular variable? The common answer is almost disappointingly simple: The choice of a particular set of measurement values is usually based on mere convenience. For example, successive integer values are often assigned to the categories of nominal and ordinal variables. But this is simply because they are easy to remember, and simpler to write than other possible values (e.g., decimals or fractions); it has nothing whatsoever to do with the magnitudes of the numbers themselves. Similarly, Americans use the Fahrenheit scale to express temperatures, and dollars to express wealth, simply because other Americans are more likely to understand those measurement schemes than they are the Celsius scales or some foreign currency. Nevertheless, the later schemes can provide equally accurate measures of temperature, wealth, or whatever. There is certainly nothing wrong in assigning numbers according to some arbitrary convenient scheme (so long as it is consistent with the assumptions about the nature of *f*). However, we can never forget that other numbers could be assigned to the same objects to convey the same information.

Optimal Scaling. In fact, there are more systematic strategies for applying numbers to objects, within the confines of any given measurement level. For example, Young (1987, p. 64) argues that "the measurement characteristics of a set of data are [not] characteristics of the data in vacuo; rather . . . the measurement characteristics depend on the interaction of the data with the model being used to analyze the data." Building upon this idea, Young suggests that numbers can be assigned to objects using a strategy that he calls "optimal scaling." According to this strategy, the measurement *characteristics* of a data set are specified a priori. However, the specific numerical *values* are obtained as part of the analysis. Specifically, the observations are assigned scores in a way that simultaneously fulfills two conditions: (1) The assigned scores fit the statistical model as well as possible; and (2) they strictly maintain the specified measurement characteristics. The optimal scaling strategy has the advantage of providing the best set of numerical assignments for the data, where "best" is defined as a least squares fit between an analytic model and a set of empirical observations. Furthermore, whereas the data's measurement characteristics must be specified prior to an analysis, the researcher can certainly vary his or her assumptions about the characteristics, and observe the effects on the analytic results. Young (1987, pp. 64-65) points out the important benefit that this provides:

> One can obtain *empirical* information about the measurement characteristics of raw data, at least within the context posed by the . . . model used in the analysis. All that has to be done is to analyze the data several times, each time using exactly the same analysis model, but making different measurement assumptions. If two (or more) of these analyses yield precisely the same results, then the appropriate measurement assumptions are the strictest ones used for the several equivalent analyses.

Thus the optimal scaling strategy explicitly incorporates the idea that all measurement is theory testing, because decisions about the measurement characteristics and the numerical assignments can both be made within the context of fitting a model to data. Therefore, it provides a means of implementing the relatively flexible view of measurement advocated in this monograph. We will pursue these ideas in greater detail in Chapter 6.

The Importance of Measurement Levels. The traditional justification for distinguishing between levels of measurement emphasizes that only certain mathematical operations are appropriate at each of the levels. Hence, only identity comparisons can be made at the nominal level, and only inequality comparisons are appropriate at the ordinal level. Comparisons involving specific numerical quantities are only possible with variables measured at the interval or ratio levels. These mathematical limitations, in turn, affect the statistical procedures that can be used in each case (Stevens, 1946). Thus the mode is the only measure of central tendency that is appropriate for nominal variables, whereas the median uses ordinal information. Of course, the mean relies on the arithmetic operations of addition and division (which require specific numerical values), so it is reserved for interval and ratio variables. Thus measurement levels are important primarily because they determine which statistics researchers can employ in their analyses.

The preceding "appropriate statistics" view is widely held, particularly among social scientists. However, it has been vigorously challenged as an unnecessary restriction (e.g., Baker, Hardyck, and Petrinovich, 1966; Gaito, 1980; Lord, 1953). The objection centers around the idea that measurement and statistical theory are two completely different things. Measurement theory is concerned with the substantive meaning underlying a set of numbers. But statistical theory is wholly focused on differences and relationships among the numbers themselves. The meanings of the numbers are entirely irrelevant to the operation of any statistical procedure. Hence any assumptions about the levels of measurement required to perform statistical operations are equally unnecessary.

Arguments over the relations between measurement and statistics are difficult to resolve, at best (Michell, 1986; Townsend and Ashby, 1984). Therefore, it is probably more useful to take a different perspective, one based upon the amount of information that is conveyed at each level. Scientists try to explain differences between empirical objects. Therefore, they are more concerned with variability in a measure, rather than the actual numeric values in the measure (e.g., Weisberg, 1991). But observed variability can arise from at least two sources: (1) the underlying substantive property of the objects — in other words, the attribute that the researcher is trying to measure; and (2) the ways that the numbers are assigned to the objects — the nature of the function mapping the observations into the real number system. As we have already seen, the levels of measurement differ among themselves with respect to the second source: Higher levels are more restrictive in the kinds of functions that can be used to assign numbers to objects. Therefore, a higher proportion of the observed variance is going to be attributable to the substantive differences among the objects, rather than the "slippage" in the numerical assignments. This, alone, justifies the use of higher measurement levels wherever possible. Within the limits imposed by measurement precision (i.e., the degree of measurement error), variables measured at higher levels convey more information about substantive differences among objects than do variables measured at lower levels.

3. DATA THEORY

Scientific investigation requires empirical observation. But, any single observation supplies a great deal of information. Some of this information is superfluous for the research at hand; therefore, it is usually ignored by the analyst. But part of the information is retained and used for investigative purposes. This latter information is what we mean by the term *data*. Data are different from observations. They consist of clearly defined pieces of information that are drawn from the observations, but interpreted in specific ways. Thus data are always a subjective creation of the analyst. Coombs (1964) provides a hypothetical example that clarifies these ideas:

> If an individual is asked whether he would vote for candidate A, the observer usually records his answer, yes or no; but we might [also measure] . . . the time it took him to answer . . . whether there was a change in respiration, or in his galvanic skin response, or what he did with his hands, and so on. From this richness, the scientist must select some few things to record. . . . These recorded observations, however, are not yet data. . . . An interpretive step on the part of the scientist . . . is required to convert the recorded observations into data. [This] involves a classification of observations in the sense that individuals and stimuli are identified and labeled, and the observations are classified in terms of a relation of some kind between individuals and stimuli, or perhaps just between stimuli. (pp. 4-5)

Data theory provides abstract models for understanding the information conveyed by real world observations. The use of such abstract models means that characteristics of data can be examined completely separately from the substantive phenomena that generated the data in the first place. This, in turn, enables the development of general guidelines for determining which analytic procedures are appropriate in any given research context.

Data as a Geometric Model

All empirical observations, regardless of subject matter, involve implicit comparisons. At the most basic level, comparisons are fundamental to perception: They enable individuals to distinguish objects from their surroundings. But to be more specific, scientific observations always compare one entity to another. Thus "the apple is red" compares "apple" against a set of colors. To say that it is red means that it is *not* green, yellow, or any other color. Similarly, the observation that "student A performs better on a test than student B" usually means that the students are compared on the basis of the number of correct answers that each received on the test. Of course, examples of empirical observations are endless; fortunately, the notion that observation involves comparison is relatively straightforward. Still, the wide variety in the *types* of observations that can occur in scientific research suggests that it would be useful to seek some overarching framework that can be used to reduce the general idea of "empirical observations" to some more manageable, comprehensible form. In other words, we are looking for an abstract model that conveys the information drawn from a set of empirical observations.

One way to model observations is to take a geometric approach. If a given observation involves a comparison between two entities, then represent the latter as points within a space. The relative positions of the two points depend on the way the analyst chooses to interpret the substantive comparison between the entities. So, "the apple is red" could mean that the "apple" point and the "red" point are relatively close to each other within the space. Or, "student A performs better than student B" might imply that the "A" point occupies a more extreme position within the space than the "B" point.

Scientific research usually relies on multiple observations pertaining to the phenomenon under investigation. Each observation is a distinct comparison between two entities; therefore, it is modeled as a separate pair of points.[6] For each observation, the analyst records a piece of information that summarizes the comparison between the entities; this, in turn, can be modeled as a comparative geometric relation between the members of the point pair. The *data* consist of the specific entities in the point pairs, along with the researcher's interpretation of the relation between the elements of each pair. Thus the nature of the data determines how the geometric model will be constructed from the empirical observations.

Note how the geometric representation of data fulfills the modeling objective mentioned earlier. The notion of point pairs is sufficiently general to encompass any kind of observation: subjects and stimuli, pairs of stimuli, pairs of subjects, a physical property of an object (e.g., its weight) and a reading on a measurement instrument (a value obtained from a scale), and so on. And as we will see below, many kinds of comparisons can be represented by a surprisingly small number of geometric relations between points.

Coombs's Theory of Data

Clyde H. Coombs developed several theories based entirely on the geometric interpretation of data. In the simplest version of his work (Coombs, Dawes, and Tversky, 1970), the two entities in a single datum can vary in two ways:

(1) The two elements in the pair can be drawn from *different sets* (e.g., a student and a test question, a consumer and a product, a stimulus and a response) or they can be drawn from the *same set* (e.g., student A and student B who take the same test, brand X and brand Y from a set of consumer products, stimulus 1 and stimulus 2 from an experimental set).

(2) The comparison between the entities in the pair involves a *dominance relation* (e.g., a student answers a test question correctly, one laboratory rat completes a maze faster than another, a stimulus magnitude exceeds a certain tick mark on a measuring instrument) or a *proximity relation* (e.g., two products share an ingredient, one member of a group selects another as a coworker, one particular response accompanies a given stimulus).

It is important to understand how the brief examples mentioned above illustrate each of the twofold distinctions. First, the reader should be able to pick out the two elements in each pair and specify whether they come from the same or different sets. This is self-explanatory in many cases. We can usually determine whether the entities belong to the same or different sets simply by considering the substantive nature of the objects: It is easy to see that subjects are fundamentally different from stimuli, whereas two test items share a common characteristic (i.e., they are both included on the test). However, there are certain situations where objects in a single substantive set of objects are analyzed as if they actually belong to two different sets. For example, an investigation of interpersonal interactions among a group of people may treat the individual subjects as if they belong to two sets simultaneously: A subject is a member of the first set when he or she initiates a contact with another subject; the person is a member of the second set when he or she is the target of a contact. Thus the distinction between one and two sets of objects is not always as straightforward as it might seem.

The second distinction between the elements of a pair is sometimes a bit confusing. Speaking very loosely, a dominance relation exists when one object possesses more or less of some characteristic than another object. For example, a primary school student possesses a certain level of arithmetic ability. At the same time, a math problem possesses a certain degree of difficulty. If the student's ability exceeds (i.e., dominates) the problem's difficulty, then he or she obtains a correct answer. Of course, the opposite is also true; if the difficulty level is greater than the ability, then an incorrect answer will be the result. Alternatively, proximity relations exist whenever two objects match or coincide with each other to a greater or lesser extent. For example, two colors that are judged to be similar to each other are proximal, whereas two colors that are dissimilar are not. Again, the difference between dominance and proximity is sometimes readily apparent from the nature of the empirical observation, as when one student successfully completes more test questions than another (dominance) or when two students complete the same test questions (proximity). But the distinction still ultimately rests with the analyst's *interpretation* of the observations, and not with the observations themselves. For example, consider an experimental subject completing some assigned task. From one perspective, this may be a dominance relation (i.e., the subject's skill level exceeds that necessary for the task). From another perspective, this may be a proximity relation (the subject's skills happen to coincide with those necessary to complete the task). These examples demonstrate once again that data are always the result of a creative step on the part of the researcher. The nature of the data is never automatically determined by any particular set of empirical observations, because the data are different from the observations themselves.

The two dichotomous distinctions are easily transformed into geometric representations.[7] The entities contained in a single observation are always modeled as a pair of points within a space. Although this space can have several dimensions, we will confine our attention in this chapter to the simplest version, a unidimensional space (or a single dimension). In any event, if the elements of the pair are from different sets, the space is often called a "joint space" because it contains two distinct sets of points. If the objects are from a single set, then the space is sometimes called a "stimulus space" or "subject space" or, more generally, an "object space." If the objects in the observation pair are connected by a dominance relation, this is reflected in the ordering of the points in the space. If one entity dominates another, its point is placed at a more extreme (usually, numerically higher) position along the dimension. On the other hand, proximity is modeled as interpoint distance. As two objects become more proximal, the distance between their two points becomes smaller, and vice versa.

Pairs of Points
in Observation

	Same Set	Different Sets
Dominance	Stimulus Comparison	Single Stimulus
Proximity	Similarities	Preferential Choice

Relation Between Points in Pair

Figure 3.1. The Four Types of Data in Coombs's Data Theory

The two dichotomous distinctions operate simultaneously to produce the four different kinds of data shown in Figure 3.1. *All* empirical observations, regardless of their substantive nature, can be classified as one of these four types. We will consider each one, in turn.

Single Stimulus Data. Here, observations are pairs of objects drawn from different sets. There is a dominance relation between the objects. Examples of single stimulus data include: students and test questions, survey respondents and the ordered categories on a rating scale, and the length of an object and the tick marks along a ruler. This third example makes the important point that virtually all physical measurement falls within the category of single stimulus data. In such cases, the two point sets are (1) the objects being measured, and (2) the calibration units on the measurement instrument. If an object is, say, four millimeters long, this means that the length dominates all the tick marks on a ruler up to the four-millimeter mark; it fails to dominate (it is dominated by) all marks that are greater than four millimeters. In general, if object A has score y on variable x, then the point for A dominates y units of a continuum corresponding to the variable x. Regardless of the substantive meaning of the observations, the geometric model for single stimulus data implies an order relation between each pair of points along the underlying dimension. To say that x dominates y implies that a point representing x is placed at a numerically larger position (i.e., farther toward the right) along a number line than the point representing y.

Stimulus Comparison Data. Here, observations involve pairs with elements drawn from the same set, with a dominance relation between them. This usually occurs when similar objects are compared to each other on the basis of some common property. Thus the data show that, say, object X has more of a given property than object Y. For example, one automobile gets better gas mileage than an other, one stimulus is more attractive than another stimulus, one task takes longer to learn than another task. Once again, each of the preceding observations consists of a dominance relation that would be modeled as an *ordering* of two points along a number line. The points would represent automobiles, stimuli, and tasks, respectively; the number lines would correspond to gas mileage, attractiveness, and time. Superficially, this situation may seem to be identical to single stimulus data. However, it is not. With single stimulus data, one type of object is compared to some other, fundamentally different, kind of object: Thus a *stimulus* is evaluated by a *response;* a *student* completes a *test item;* an *object* possesses x units of some *characteristic;* and so on. Here, with stimulus comparison data, the comparison is made between two similar objects (i.e., they are drawn from the same set). In one limited sense, the "end result" is the same in each case. For both types of data, the information contained in an empirical observation implies an ordering of a point pair along a number line. But the information used to construct this geometric representation is very different in each case.

Similarities Data. Observations are modeled here as pairs of entities drawn from the same set, with a proximity relation between them. As the name implies, the most obvious substantive example of such data involves similarity. As a pair of stimuli are judged to be more or less similar, then the proximity between them increases or decreases, respectively. Other examples of similarities data might include certain kinds of correlation between two variables; the degree to which two stimulus objects are confused with each other by a panel of judges, the degree to which two subjects exhibit the same behavior, and so on. Here, the empirical comparison between two objects is modeled as a *distance* between a pair of points. It does not say anything at all about the *ordering* of the points within the space.

Preferential Choice Data. These observations are represented by pairs of objects drawn from different sets, with a proximity relation between them. The most obvious example of such data is actual preference behavior. Thus the more a given subject "likes" or "prefers" a particular stimulus, then the greater the proximity between the subject and the stimulus. But this type of data is far more general than the name might seem to imply. It can be appropriate for virtually any situation where elements of one set are matched to elements of another set. Therefore, this kind of data is appropriate for labeling behavior: If object X is labeled A, B, and C, but not D, E, and F, then the A, B, and C labels are more proximal to X than are the labels D, E, and F. Preferential choice data can also be extracted from situations where stimuli are rated according to the degree that they exhibit certain characteristics: The more a stimulus possesses a characteristic, the greater the proximity between that stimulus and that characteristic. Geometrically, the proximities are represented as distances between points, within a joint space. Increasing proximity between a subject and stimulus (or object and label, or whatever) corresponds to decreasing distance between the subject point and the stimulus point. As with similarities data, the information contained in any single preferential choice data supplies no information about the relative *ordering* of the subject and the stimulus within the space.

Figure 3.2 gives some examples to show how empirical observations can be transformed into the four types of data. Note that in several cases, a single *observation* is interpreted as several *data*. For each datum, the figure identifies the pair of entities contained in that datum, the relation between the pair, and a possible geometric representation of their points along a number line. Note that several geometric models are shown for the similarities data and the preferential choice data. This is done to reiterate the idea that proximities only provide information about distances; they do not suggest any ordering of the points.

Although it is probably already clear from the examples, it is important to emphasize again that the names given to the four types of data are chosen for convenience only. Each data type can subsume a variety of substantively different observations. In certain cases, the names are actually somewhat misleading. Thus "single stimulus" data still involve two

	Empirical Observation	Point Pairs	Relation Between Points	Possible Geometric Model
Single Stimulus Data	Student A answers Question 1 correctly	Student A, Question 1	"answers correctly" implies ">"	A ⊢——•—— 1
	Book X weighs 2 pounds	Book X, Weight (in pounds)	"weighs C" implies "> C and < C"	X 1 2 3 1b. lbs. lbs.
Stimulus Comparison Data	Team A wins game over Team B, loses to Team C	2 observ'ns: Teams A & B, Teams A & C	"Wins" implies ">" "loses" implies "<"	B A C
	Food X tastes saltier than Food Y	Food X, Food Y	"Tastes saltier" implies ">"	Y X
Similarities Data	Senators X & Y vote alike more than Senators W & Z	2 observ'ns: Sens. X & Y, Sens. W & Z	"Vote alike" implies smaller distance	X Y W Z or W X Y Z or Z Y X Z
	Cake is more like a cookie than like bread	2 observ'ns: Cake (C) & cookie (K), Cake (C) & Bread (B)	"More like" implies smaller distance	K C B or B K C
Preferential Choice Data	Child A likes ice cream better than carrots	2 observ'ns: Child A & ice cream (I), Child A & carrots (C)	"Likes" implies smaller distance	I A C A I C C A I
	The apple is red, but not green or yellow	3 observ'ns: Apple (A) & red (R), A & green (G), A & Yellow (Y)	"Is" implies smaller distance than "is not"	Y G R A G Y A R Y R A G

Figure 3.2. Examples of Observations for the Four Types of Data

sets of objects, and the researcher may choose to regard both of them as "stimuli" for analytic purposes (e.g., the researcher may want simultaneously to order students on the basis of test performance, and to test items on the basis of their difficulty). In the same vein, "preferential choice" data need not have anything to do with actual preferences at all (as in the case of attaching labels to stimuli). The naming of the four types of data should be regarded as nothing more than a shorthand device. The names simply stand for different kinds of geometric relations implied by empirical observations. They say nothing whatsoever about the substantive processes that generate the data.

An Alternative Theory of Data

There are several other ways to model empirical observations in addition to the fourfold classification system presented here (e.g., Coombs, 1953, 1964; Coxon, 1982; Roskam, 1977; Shepard, 1972). Recently, Carroll and Arabie (1980) and Young (1987) have classified types of data according to the overall shape of the data matrix, rather than the geometric models used to represent the cells within the data matrix. This alternative data theory (which we will identify as CAY, for Carroll, Arabie, and Young) nicely complements Coombs's work, and it is becoming increasingly visible in the scaling literature. The central ideas involve the numbers of *ways* and *modes* contained in a data matrix. The term *ways* refers to the dimensions of the matrix. The *modes* of a data matrix correspond to the number of distinct, different kinds of objects that are represented by the ways of the matrix. Each way of a data matrix has its own number of *levels,* corresponding to the number of entities in that object set. Thus the ways define the overall shape of the data matrix, the modes determine the interpretation of the objects, and the levels specify the size of the matrix.

In any data set, there is a minimum of two ways, because an observation always involves a comparison between two objects. The number of modes depends on the type of objects. For example, there are two modes when survey respondents answer a set of questionnaire items; of course, the modes are the respondents and the items, respectively. If there are N respondents and K items, then the first way of the data matrix has N levels, whereas the second way has K levels. As a different example, consider a data set containing pairwise comparisons among a set of K stimuli (e.g., which stimulus in the pair is more attractive?). These observations would probably be represented in a matrix with two ways (corresponding to the two stimuli within each pair) and a single mode (the stimuli, because they are the only objects involved in the comparisons); each way would have K levels, because the stimuli are compared against each other.

Two-way, two-mode data matrices are probably the most common type. But the CAY data theory can handle more complex situations very easily. If each observation is replicated several times, then there are at least three ways in the matrix, with the third way corresponding to the replications. Once again, the modes depend on the nature of the observations. N respondents answering K questions at each of M time points would produce three modes: Respondents (N levels); questions (K levels); and time points (M levels). Repeated observations (at M time points) of pairwise comparisons among K stimuli would also generate a matrix with three ways. However, there would only be two distinct modes: the K stimuli; and the M replications. An even more complicated situation arises when N judges rate K stimuli according to Q different attributes on each of M different occasions. In this case, the data matrix would probably contain four ways and four modes, corresponding to: judges (N levels); stimuli (K levels): attributes (Q levels); and occasions (M levels). In general, the number of modes can never exceed the number of ways, although it can be less. Figure 3.3 shows several examples of data sets organized on the basis of this theory.

It is important to emphasize that the type of data matrix appropriate for any given situation depends entirely upon the analyst's *interpretation* of the observations, rather than on the substantive nature of the entities involved in the empirical observations. Accordingly, the number and type of empirically distinguishable entities contained in the observations may or may not correspond to the shape and size of the data matrix. For example, a researcher studying intercity travel among K cities could arrange the observations in a two-way matrix, with K levels (one for each city) in each way. If the researcher is only interested in the *total* amount of travel between each pair of cities (e.g., the number of people who reported driving from city A to city B *or* from B to A), then there is only one mode, corresponding to the cities. On the other hand, the researcher may want to examine the *direction* of travel between cities. In this case, it is important to distinguish between departure points and destination points. The two ways of the data matrix would still each contain the same K cities. *Analytically,* however, the researcher would distinguish between departure cities and destination cities, and treat them as distinct objects. To extend this example a bit further, the researcher may have data

1) N Subjects' scores on K variables: 2 Ways, 2 Modes (Subjects and Variables)

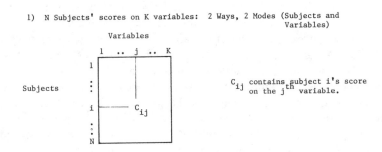

C_{ij} contains subject i's score on the jth variable.

2) Comparisons among K objects, repeated N times: 3 Ways, 2 Modes (objects and replications)

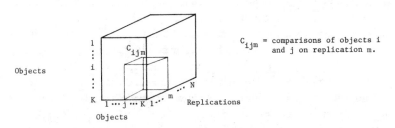

C_{ijm} = comparisons of objects i and j on replication m.

3) All pairwise comparisons among K objects, on each of N·traits, measured on P occasions: 4 Ways, 3 Modes (objects, traits, occasions)

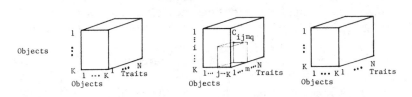

C_{ijmq} = comparisons between objects i and j, on trait 1, measured on occasion q.

Figure 3.3. Examples of Date Matrices, Carroll-Arabie-Young Theory of Data

collected separately for Q several different forms of transportation (e.g., private automobile, public surface transportation, and air transportation), over M different years. Assuming that we still distinguish between departure and destination cities, these observations could generate a four-way, four-mode, matrix of K departure cities by K destination cities by Q forms of transportation by M years. Alternatively, there may be no substantive reason to distinguish between different forms of transportation, or different years (even though the information has been collected). In that case, the latter would simply be taken as repeated observations on the amount of travel between cities. The resultant data matrix would still have four ways, but now there are only three distinct modes: departure cities (K levels) by destination cities (K levels) by replications (QM levels). Once again, the data are treated as an abstract model extracted from the observations; as such, the characteristics of the data are entirely independent from the substantive properties of the observations themselves.

Although the CAY data theory takes a different focus, it is entirely consistent with the Coombs fourfold classification. Single stimulus data and preferential choice data both produce matrices with (at least) two ways and two modes. The differences between them involve the comparative relation that holds across the modes: It is a dominance relation in the first case, and a proximity relation in the second case. Stimulus comparison data and similarities data both generate two-way matrices with a single mode. Again, they differ because one involves a dominance relation, and one a proximity relation. Of course, it is possible to have replicated observations for any of these kinds of data. In that case, the number of ways and modes in the data matrix will increase accordingly. It is often useful to think in terms of both of these data theories, rather than rely on one by itself. Each one illuminates a different aspect of the information obtained from empirical observations.

It is also important to recognize that measurement characteristics and data characteristics involve two separate sets of assumptions that a researcher must make about his or her empirical observations. They involve two models that are applied simultaneously, in order to produce the raw material for subsequent analyses. However, these two models are entirely independent of each other. The CAY theory makes this explicit by stating that the data are defined by the combination of the measurement characteristics and the shape of the data matrix. But the distinction is also relevant for Coombs's theory: The fourfold classification of data is entirely independent of the level of measurement. It is possible to have ordinal, interval, ratio, and sometimes even nominal versions of each of the four data types. The important idea here is that the measurement level concerns the type of function used to attach numbers to the geometric relations implied by the data. This is completely separate from the nature of the geometric relation itself.

The Importance of Data Theory

Data theory clarifies the nature of the information that is brought into an analysis context. How that information is used depends upon the researcher's intentions. If the objective is strictly to test a statistical model, then the data characteristics are probably of little interest in themselves. Most of the "standard" statistical procedures require a two-way, two-mode matrix of single stimulus data. Thus a regression model assumes a rectangular data set with numerical entries, expressing the scores assigned to a set of observations on a set of variables.

In contrast, a scaling analysis is usually more directly concerned with the nature of the information contained in the data matrix. From the perspective of the CAY theory, the objective is usually to reduce the size of the data matrix, while still maintaining the essential character of the variability among the objects represented in the matrix. In Coombs's data theory, observations are modeled geometrically as points within a space. Each datum can be viewed as an incomplete, imperfect manifestation or replication of the overall space, in the sense that it provides information about the relative locations of a single pair of points. A scaling procedure is used to combine the incomplete pieces of information from the separate observations in order to estimate a single, relatively complete geometric model — the entire space, containing all of the relevant point locations.

In the chapter, we have seen that a theory of data provides systematic guidelines for interpreting empirical observations. This is important for organizing the information in ways that are suitable for subsequent analyses. In Chapter 5, I will argue that the selection of any analytic strategy must be largely based upon the nature of the data that are available for analysis. Therefore, it is probably no exaggeration to say that data theory is one of the most fundamental components of scientific investigation.

4. DIMENSIONALITY

The concept of *dimensionality* is used very loosely in everyday conversation. For example, a person with a very rigid outlook on life is sometimes said to possess a "unidimensional personality." Or dimensionality is sometimes equated with the degree of simplicity/complexity in some endeavor (e.g., a difficult or ambiguous problem is sometimes said to have a "multidimensional solution"). Neither of these usages is incorrect, in any way. But for purposes of measurement and scaling, we must be more specific.

Dimensionality as Variation Among Objects

From a substantive perspective, the dimensionality of a set of objects is simply defined as the number of separate and interesting sources of variation among the objects. Thus an assessment of dimensionality requires the researcher to consider two questions simultaneously: First, in how many ways do a set of objects differ among themselves? Second, of the differences that do exist, how many are important — that is, relevant to the goals of the scientific investigation?

Although this substantive interpretation of dimensionality is relatively simple, it does have several important consequences. First, the dimensionality of an object set is tied to substantive characteristics of those objects. In some cases, the nature of the characteristics is immediately obvious; in other cases, it may be less so. Second, specifying dimensionality is a positive step on the part of the researcher. The dimensions themselves have no inherent, substantive reality. They merely simplify the characteristics of a set of objects, in order to make them more comprehensible for analytic purposes. In this way, a dimensional representation of an object set is always a model of the objects, rather than an immutable property of the objects. Third, dimensionality is usually context specific; the number of dimensions assumed to exist among an object set depends upon the ways the objects are examined. For some purposes, they could be regarded as unidimensional; for other purposes, the researcher may find some multidimensional representation of the same object set more appropriate. There is absolutely nothing wrong with this, so long as the selected dimensionality corresponds to all of the *relevant* sources of variation among the objects. But it is always the researcher who decides what is relevant in the first place.

A few examples may help to clarify these ideas. In some research settings, the analyst actually creates the stimulus objects that will be examined. In such cases, he or she can determine the dimensionality of the objects a priori. Thus an experiment on perceptual acuity might present subjects with pictures of geometric figures that have differing shapes, heights, and widths. The figures vary among themselves in three ways, so there are three dimensions underlying that particular set of objects. Assume that the experimenter instructs the subjects to categorize the figures, and that all of the subjects do so on the basis of the shapes only; they ignore any size differences across the figures. In this case, there is only a single dimension of variability among the objects. Which of these dimensionalities is the "correct" one? The answer is either one. If the experimenter is interested in the physical characteristics of the figures, then the three-dimensional view of the figures is necessary. If the behavior of the subjects is the primary focus, then the unidimensional interpretation is probably sufficient.

Outside a laboratory setting, researchers usually have very little control over dimensionality. And most of the objects that social scientists examine are inherently complex (people, organizations, political systems, etc.), meaning precisely that they differ in many ways simultaneously. Therefore, virtually everything *could* be viewed in multidimensional terms. But recall that dimensionality involves the *important* sources of variability underlying a set of objects. In any particular research context, the number of important differences is likely to be far less than the total number of differences. And once again, it is always the analyst who defines what is important. For example, a researcher might be examining the degree to which work groups achieve their goals. If he or she finds that the only important factor is, say, the degree of interpersonal contact among group members, then the groups would vary only along this single dimension. On the other hand, goal achievement may depend upon the nature of the goals along with the degree of intragroup contact; accordingly, the objects would be regarded as two-dimensional. In either case, the researcher would probably disregard the other ways that groups differed among themselves; for purposes of the analysis, the objects would only differ in one or two *relevant* ways.

Dimensionality as a Mathematical Model

Let us now move from the preceding substantive definition of dimensionality to a more mathematical conception. For each source of variability, numbers are used to differentiate between the objects. Thus each source of variation can be represented by its own number line. The number lines can be used as coordinate axes in a space. The objects under investigation are modeled as points within the space, with their locations determined by their positions along each of the coordinate axes. If the objects vary in only one way, then a single number line will suffice to display the differences between them. Hence, the phenomenon is uni-dimensional. If the objects differ in two ways simultaneously, then two number lines will be necessary and the variability is regarded as two-dimensional, and so on.

In general, the dimensionality of a set of objects refers to the minimum number of coordinates required to locate uniquely the set of points representing the objects. If there are too few coordinates for each point, then some of the variability between the objects cannot be incorporated into the model. If there are too many coordinates, then some of the information is redundant. For example, consider Figures 4.1 and 4.2. The upper half of Figure 4.1 shows a set of geometric shapes. In the lower half of the figure, points representing each of these shapes are plotted, with their locations determined by their values on each of two coordinate axes. The horizontal axis corresponds to the widths of the figures, and the vertical axis corresponds to their heights. Note that both axes are neces-sary to locate the points uniquely, because several figures have identical widths but different heights, and vice versa. If only one axis were used (say, width), then the variability in heights could not be shown, and the differences between the objects would not be adequately represented. Thus these objects vary in two dimensions. Figure 4.2 shows a different situation. Again, the upper half of the figure shows a series of geometric figures, which are plotted as points in the lower half. However, in this case, one of the coordinate axes is redundant; the figures are all squares, so the lengths of the sides do not vary independently of each other. As shown in the lower half of the figure, the points all fall along a single line, even though they are graphed using two coordinates each. Thus the two-dimensional model contains unnecessary complexity. As a simpler alternative, it would be perfectly adequate to use a single coordinate axis, representing the areas of the figures. The latter model still summarizes all of the variability among the squares. Accordingly, a unidimensional representation uniquely locates these objects with respect to each other.

Physical Versus Conceptual Dimensions

From the preceding description, dimensions seem to be a way of drawing a "picture" that represents the objects. It is often convenient to

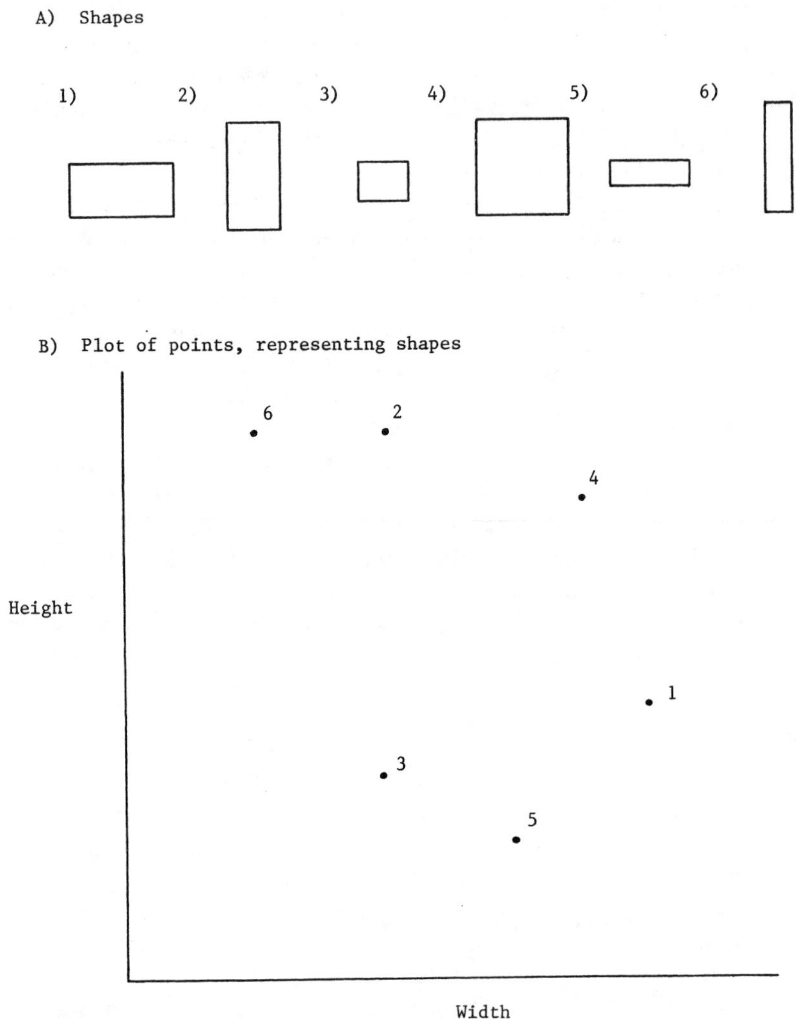
A) Shapes
1)
2)
3)
4)
5)
6)
B) Plot of points, representing shapes
6
2
4
1
3
5
Height
Width

Figure 4.1. Geometric Shapes, Plotted in Two-Dimensional Space

think of dimensions in such graphic terms, precisely because doing so provides an easy way of visualizing the differences between the objects. But what happens if the objects vary in more than two or three distinct

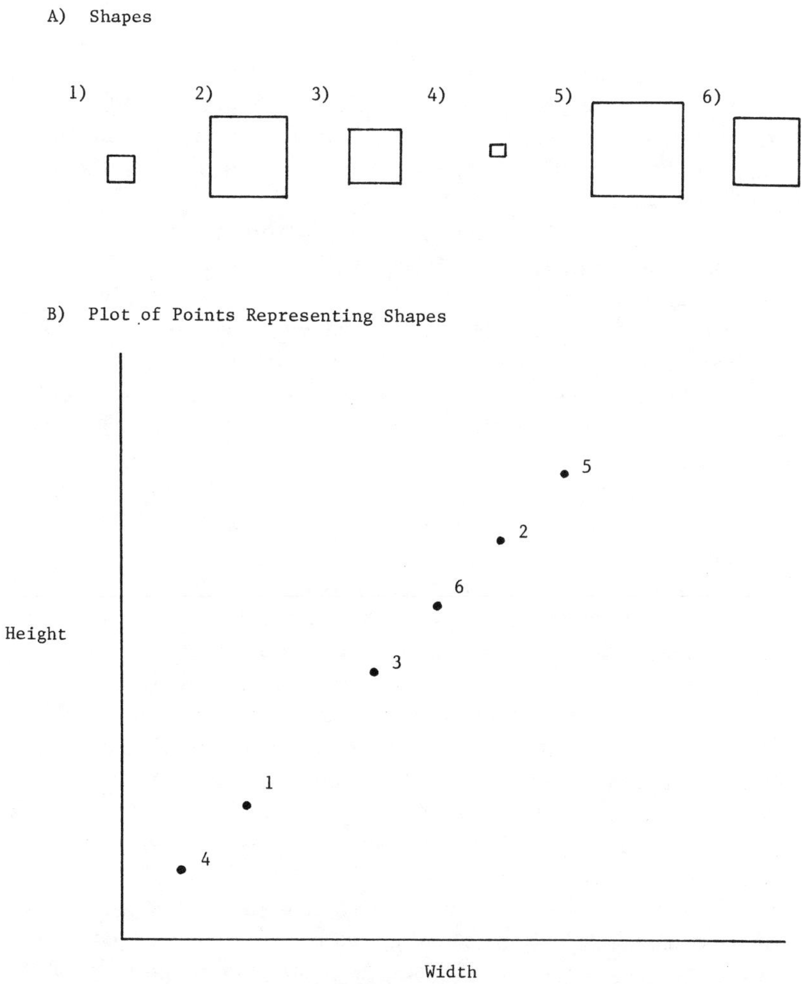

A) Shapes

B) Plot of Points Representing Shapes

Figure 4.2. Plot of Geometric Shapes, Including a Redundant Dimension

ways? We can construct physical models depicting one-, two-, or three-dimensional sets of objects, but we certainly cannot do so with four-dimensional phenomena! Of course, we could still construct a physical model showing *part* of the four-dimensional space; that is, any one, two, or three of the dimensions at a time. This may be a helpful step, but it would only provide an incomplete representation of the objects. And creating a physical model is unnecessary. The space containing the points is, itself, defined by the set of coordinates for each of the objects. The latter are completely sufficient for locating or "mapping" the objects with respect to each other. A physical depiction of the point locations (i.e., a map) is, strictly speaking, merely redundant information once we have the actual coordinate values.

It is essential to distinguish between *physical* dimensions and their separate, *conceptual* existence. There is no reason to limit ourselves to a maximum of three sources of variability among objects simply because we cannot draw a picture of four. The inability to construct some exact physical counterpart to a four-dimensional space does not make it any less real than three or fewer dimensions. Indeed, reliance on graphical depiction of dimensions can actually hinder understanding of the phenomena under investigation.

The latter point is probably made most effectively in Edwin Abbott's (1983) tale of *Flatland*. Flatland is a two-dimensional world — a plane. Its inhabitants are geometrical figures who live on the surface of the plane. They have their own stratification system (based upon the number of sides possessed by each geometric figure) and social norms (e.g., women, who are straight lines, must be continually on their guard to avoid damaging male, solid figures). One day, an inhabitant of this world (A Square, the narrator of *Flatland*) is visited by a creature from another world — a sphere — who tries to explain the existence of a third dimension. The sphere presents a variety of arguments, but the square will not be convinced that another dimension exists. After all, he cannot see it, and everything with which he is familiar functions perfectly well in the two-dimensional world. The square only recognizes the existence of the third dimension when the sphere bumps him off the plane. Unfortunately, the resultant insight leads to ostracization for the square: His fellow Flatlanders reject his strange ideas about the third dimension, and the sphere abandons him when he suggests that there may be even more than three dimensions.

Flatland is an amusing fable, but it has a moral that is very important for our present purposes. Weisberg (1974) states that it "serves to emphasize how our inability to comprehend fully the basics of geometry limits our understanding of scaling. Like the square, we must be lifted out of our Flatland if we are to perceive the variety of dimensional forms." Dimensions can have a strictly conceptual existence, with no physical counterpart whatsoever. From this perspective, dimensionality simply refers to the number of coordinates required to locate uniquely a set of objects relative to each other. Assessing dimensionality is a mapping process, although the map is purely conceptual rather than physical in nature.

The substantive and mathematical perspectives on dimensionality coincide in their respective emphases on the number of *important* sources of variability among objects, and on the *minimum* number of coordinates needed to map the objects. In each case, the goal is to obtain the most parsimonious representation of the objects under consideration. An example illustrates these ideas very nicely. Consider a map of a geographic area. Maps are quintessential examples of dimensional models, because they provide geometric representations of the physical world. But the dimensionality of the model depends upon the purpose of the map. A topographical engineer would most likely require a map that shows all three dimensions of the surface of the Earth (i.e., latitude, longitude, and height above sea level). In contrast, road maps usually only portray the first two of these dimensions. The implicit assumption is that, for most motorists, the third dimension need not be taken into account when the map is used. The important point to be drawn from this example is that dimensionality involves determining the number of important differences among a set of objects. And the definition of *important* depends entirely upon the context.

Scaling and Dimensional Analysis

We can use the ideas about dimensionality to provide a geometric interpretation of any scaling procedure. Basically, all scaling strategies seek to represent objects as points within a space. The geometric differences in the point locations are related to the substantive differences among the objects. The dimensions of the space correspond to the sources of variability underlying the objects. All scaling procedures share this common goal. Of course, the way that one proceeds from observations, to data, and finally to the geometric representation differs from one scaling strategy to the next. We will take up this problem, in detail, in the next chapter. For now, let us address some general considerations about scaling procedures and the dimensionality of the objects that are scaled.

In many situations, the sources of variability among the objects are known beforehand. Therefore, the overall structure of the dimensional space (particularly the number of dimensions) can be specified by the researcher before the task of locating the object points is begun. This is the case for physical measurement and virtually any other context where objects are compared on the basis of known criteria. On the other hand, many scaling procedures are intended to *identify* the number of dimensions that are required, along with locating the positions of the objects along the coordinate axes. Hence they are often called "dimensional analysis" strategies. This is particularly important in the social and behavioral sciences, because researchers often do not have a priori knowledge about the underlying sources of empirical variation in their observations.

The Two Uses of a Scaling Procedure. Most scaling procedures can be used in two different ways. First, a scaling procedure can be used as a *scaling criterion* to ascertain whether a particular dimensional structure accurately represents an empirical set of data. Often, the question is simply, "How many dimensions are needed to distinguish between these observations?" The second usage occurs after the researcher has decided that a particular dimensional structure is appropriate. In that case, the procedure can be used as a *scaling technique,* to measure the objects with respect to the dimensions. Here, the objective is to find specific sets of coordinate values for each of the object points in the geometric scaling solution.

It is important to emphasize that most modern scaling procedures can be simultaneously employed as a criterion and a technique. The goodness of fit measure for a scaling procedure is used to assess the fit of the data to a particular dimensional structure, thereby serving as the scaling criterion. And the scaled *values* given to the observations are the end result of the scaling technique. The distinction between a criterion and a technique depends on the way the researcher chooses to interpret scaling errors.

Interpreting Scaling Errors. The geometric structures generated by scaling procedures rarely fit the data perfectly; in other words, there is usually some discrepancy between the point locations and the empirical objects. Any such discrepancies are called *scaling errors.* The nature of an "error" depends upon the specific scaling procedure — we will examine various forms of scaling errors in the next chapter. In any event, these errors have two main sources. First, they may reflect the presence of an inappropriate scaling model. Either the dimensionality is wrong, or the geometric model is inconsistent with the empirical observations. If the researcher interprets the errors this way, then he or she is applying a scaling criterion.

Second, scaling errors may simply be "fluctuations" that occur because of measurement errors, sampling errors, or stochastic factors affecting the observations. If the researcher uses this interpretation, then he or she is explicitly accepting the dimensional structure; the procedure is used solely as a scaling technique. Indeed, the major objective of a scaling technique is to eliminate the effects of these kinds of errors and produce a set of numbers that best represents the variability among the objects.[8]

The researcher can interpret errors in either of the two ways. How, then, does one decide on the interpretation of the errors in any particular scaling analysis? In most cases, the answer hinges on the *amount* of error that occurs in a given scaling solution. Stated simply, a small amount of error is usually attributed to relatively unimportant fluctuations, whereas a large amount of error is often viewed as a threat to the validity of the particular scaling model as applied to the given data set. The amount of error in a scaling solution is measured by the goodness of fit statistic for the scaling procedure.

The interpretation of scaling errors is important, because it has implications for the kind of information that can be drawn from the scaling results. Thus the scaling criterion answers substantive questions about the ways that objects differ among themselves, whereas the scaling technique provides measurement of previously ascertained object attributes (i.e., to what extent do the objects vary on each characteristic that distinguishes them?).

Multidimensionality and Multiple Unidimensionality. When a researcher employs a procedure as a scaling criterion, it is often useful to obtain results for several different dimensional structures. Usually, one starts with the simplest geometric representation of the objects — a single dimension. If the data are consistent with this model (i.e., the magnitude of the scaling errors are relatively small), then the criterion has been met. But if the data do not fit a unidimensional structure, then the next step is to try a two-dimensional solution. Once again, if the fit improves to a satisfactory level, the criterion part of the analysis can stop here. But if there is still an unacceptably high amount of error, then higher dimensional solutions can be tried. The underlying assumption with this approach is that a single characteristic *might* be leading to the observed variability among the objects under investigation; if so, then the later can be modeled as points along a single number line. If not, then the variability is attributable to the existence of several characteristics operating simultaneously. The latter situation is incorporated into a multidimensional geometric model, because all of the coordinates are used to establish the relative locations of the object points.

This "progression" from a unidimensional solution to increasingly complex multidimensional solutions is a standard strategy in commonly used scaling approaches like factor analysis and multidimensional scaling. However, van Schuur (1984, 1988) points out that multidimensional models involve certain assumptions that do not pertain to the unidimensional case. For example, multidimensional solutions assume that all of the dimensions operate simultaneously in contributing to the observed differences between the scaled objects. And, each object must be given a coordinate on every dimension contained in the space.

Van Schuur points out that these assumptions can be problematic. Even if a set of objects possesses K "objective" characteristics, there is no particular reason that *all* of the characteristics are used to differentiate among all of the objects. For example, if subjects are asked their preferences among a set of fruit drinks, they may use taste characteristics for some of the drinks, and color for other drinks. If so, then one dimension (taste, perhaps sweet versus tart) is appropriate for the first set of drinks, whereas an entirely separate dimension underlies the second set (color, such as orange versus yellow or pink).

In order to model this situation, the analyst could test for the presence of *multiple unidimensional representations* within a single set of objects. Essentially, this entails seeking subsets of the objects; within each subset, the objective is to fit a unidimensional structure (Guttman, 1945). This approach often generates several dimensions for a single data set. However, the results are not really multidimensional in the usual sense of the term, because there is only a single dimension relevant to each of the subsets.

Several scaling procedures can be used to identify subsets of stimulus objects, thereby enabling the researcher to test for the presence of multiple dimensions (as opposed to a single, multidimensional solution). Overall, this approach seems to have been more popular in the European research community than in the United States. Nevertheless, the procedures are becoming more widely known (e.g., Mokken and Lewis, 1982; Niemoller and van Schuur, 1983), so future applications will probably be more widespread. The multiple unidimensional scaling approaches provide an attractive means of integrating heterogeneity in empirical observations with parsimonious scaling solutions. As such, they are a useful alternative to relatively complex, multidimensional models.

Scaling Results and Interpreting Dimensions

A scaling procedure applied to a data set will virtually always produce a geometric structure. However, the scaling procedure cannot, in any way, provide insights about the *meaning* of the results. Only the analyst can determine whether the dimensions of the spatial structure correspond to substantively interesting characteristics of the objects. It is always important to remember that the dimensions in any scaling solution are merely coordinate systems used to locate a set of points. As such, they may or may not have substantive meaning. The researcher must resist the temptation to force a meaning onto a dimension simply because the dimension exists. Doing so can produce invalid or even nonsensical results. If the locations of a set of points cannot be *readily* interpreted in terms of one or more substantive characteristics of the objects, then serious consideration must be given to the possibility that the variability in the observations simply does not conform to a single, systematic pattern. Similarly, as the number of dimensions required to obtain a reasonable fit increases (in other words, the ratio of the number of dimensions to the number of objects approaches 1.0), we must begin to question whether there really is a structure underlying the objects in the first place.

Finally, even though the number of dimensions underlying a set of objects is not constrained by the limitations of three-dimensional space, the visual nature of many scaling results is often advantageous for interpretation purposes. Therefore, scaling solutions in spaces of low dimensionality are almost always preferred over those with many dimensions. This is certainly consistent with the overall scientific objective of parsimonious explanation. However, it goes beyond this. Stated simply, a picture *is* often worth a thousand words. Visual inspection of scaling results often allows researchers to discern patterns in objects that would not necessarily be found through other methods. And visual displays are almost always easier to communicate than numerical matrices, even when they contain exactly the same information. Thus practical considerations push analysts toward solutions with three or fewer dimensions. However, this may change as computer graphics capabilities improve. New methods of display may permit analysts to "move" through subspaces of high-dimensional spaces, thereby enabling more effective comprehension of complicated scaling solutions. Young (1987) anticipates that future innovations in scaling technology will be heavily influenced by developments in computer graphics for exactly these reasons.

5. DATA THEORY AND SCALING METHODS

The main purpose for a theory of data is to rationalize the use of scaling procedures. In other words, there are many different scaling methods available to the researcher. But which one is appropriate in any given situation? Data theory is intended to bring a comprehensive perspective to bear on this question. The choice of a scaling procedure always depends upon the researcher's interpretation of the observations — that is, the nature of the data.

In this chapter, we will examine the various types of data, and discuss some of the scaling procedures that are appropriate for each one. Note that the emphasis will be on scaling *models* rather than scaling *techniques*. That is, we will focus on abstract representations of variability within observations, rather than the specific details involved in constructing these representations. For the latter, readers will be referred to other sources, such as the appropriate volumes in this monograph series.

Single Stimulus Data

Single stimulus data are, by far, the most common of the four types. Therefore, many different scaling procedures have been devised to handle them. We will examine three models in this section: the summated rating model, the cumulative model, and the factor analysis model.

Summated Rating Scales. Summated rating scales simplify the representation of empirical observations by summing across the levels in at least one of the ways of a multiway, multimode data matrix. Figure 5.1 shows the most common situation: An N by K matrix is scaled by summing across the columns, within rows of the matrix. This results in the N by 1 matrix of empirical scale score for the objects represented by the rows. There are several versions of summated rating scales; the best known are Likert scales and Thurstone's method of equal-appearing intervals (McIver and Carmines, 1981). Although these are usually treated as different

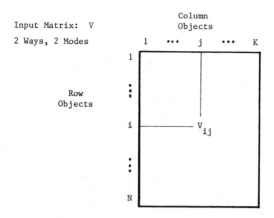

Input Matrix: V
2 Ways, 2 Modes

Column Objects

Row Objects

V_{ij} shows degree to which object i dominates object j.

Scaling Model: Points for the N objects located along dimension by summing across K objects, within each row.

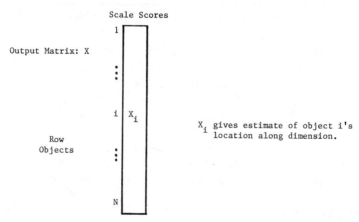

Scale Scores

Output Matrix: X

Row Objects

X_i gives estimate of object i's location along dimension.

Figure 5.1. Summated Rating Scale

scaling *techniques,* they are actually different manifestations of the same basic model.[9]

From a geometric perspective, the summated rating approach assumes that one set of points varies systematically with respect to the dimension, whereas the second set of points fluctuates randomly. For each object in the first point set, we sum across all of the objects in the second point set, so that the fluctuations cancel each other out, thereby providing an accurate estimate of the first point's location along the underlying dimension. Note that the points representing the objects in the nonscaled set are not fixed along the dimension; they can vary markedly from one row of the data matrix to the next.

From a measurement perspective, the individual items that are summed to produce the scale are ordinal-level functions of the latent dimension. In other words, the numeric values assigned to the rows of the data matrix are all monotonically related to the underlying characteristic. Summing across the items implies summing across the functions, as well. The summed monotone functions should be *linear,* because the idiosyncracies of the item-specific monotone functions should cancel each other out. And, as explained back in Chapter 2, if there is a specific function (linear, in this case) between the underlying characteristic and an empirical set of numeric assignments, then interval-level measurement has been achieved.

The summated rating model depends entirely on the assumption of random fluctuations across the items that are summed to create the scale. The criteria established for selecting items used in Thurstone and Likert scales (e.g., Edwards, 1957) can be viewed as strategies for trying to insure the randomness of interitem differences. If this assumption is met, then the summated rating approach is a very powerful scaling technique. However, this same assumption leads to the two limitations of the summated rating model.

First, the method assumes that *all* errors are attributable to random fluctuations in one set of points. However, they could actually occur for other reasons, such as the simultaneous influence of several underlying dimensions. But the summated rating model dismisses the possibility of multidimensionality on a priori grounds. In strictly practical terms, this means that the scale could appear to fit the data quite well (i.e., the reliability coefficient would take on a value close to 1.0), even though the "true" sources of variation stem from several underlying dimensions. Accordingly, the summated rating approach is very useful as a scaling technique, but poor as a scaling criterion.

The second limitation of the summated rating approach is that it only scales a single set of points, out of the two sets that always constitute single stimulus data. This must be the case, because the second point set is only assumed to vary randomly; therefore, precise estimates for these items' locations would be meaningless. Exactly *which* point set is scaled depends entirely upon the researcher's assumptions about the data and the analytic objectives. It is possible to scale subjects, while assuming that items are randomly different replications (as in the Likert scaling approach), but it is equally possible to scale items, by assuming that subjects only differ randomly with respect to the items (as in Thurstone's equal-appearing intervals approach). In any event, the ability to "collapse" one of the ways of the data matrix presupposes that any differences across levels within that way are uninteresting in substantive terms.

Cumulative Scales. In contrast to the preceding approach, the cumulative scaling model does locate both sets of points along the underlying dimension. This is accomplished by using a more stringent scaling model. The most common version of the cumulative model is a Guttman scale (McIver and Carmines, 1981), which is usually applied to a rectangular data matrix showing N subjects' responses to K dichotomous items (see Figure 5.2). The items and the subjects are both assumed to occupy fixed positions along the underlying dimension. This assumption, combined with the dominance relationship implied by single stimulus data, leads to an ordering of subject and item points based upon the cumulation of responses. A cumulative scale simplifies the information contained in the data by reducing the single N by K input matrix to two separate vectors: An N by 1 vector of subject scale locations, and a K by 1 vector of the item scale locations.

In geometric terms, each cell entry in the dichotomous data matrix provides information about a single subject-item point pair. If the cell entry is 1 then the subject point is located to the right of (i.e., it dominates) the item point along the underlying dimension. If the entry is 0 then the item point is located to the right of the subject point (that is, the item dominates the subject). Each point is located along the dimension by summing the number of 1s contained within its row or column of the data matrix. Thus the larger the number of positive responses given by a subject, the farther to the right that point is located, because it dominates a larger number of items. And the larger the number of positive responses given to an item, the farther to the left that point is located, because the item is dominated by a larger number of subjects.

A Guttman scale of dichotomous data is the simplest operationalization of the cumulative scaling model. But the model can be generalized to

Input Matrix: V

2 Ways, 2 Modes

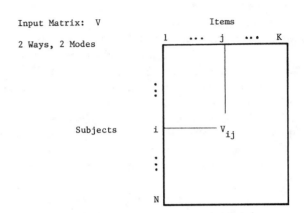

V_{ij} scored "1" if i dominates j; "0" if j dominates i.

Scaling Model: N subjects' points ordered along the dimension according to number of stimuli they dominate. K item points ordered along dimension according to number of subjects that dominate each one.

Output Matrices:

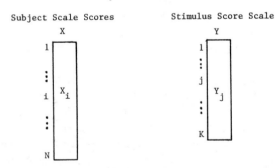

X_i = Number of distinct item cutting points located to left of subject i, along dimension.

Y_j = Number of distinct subject points located to left of item cutting point.

Figure 5.2. Cumulative (Guttman) Scale

handle a variety of other situations. For example, the cumulative approach can easily be adapted for polychotomous, ordinal items (Coombs, 1964; Edwards, 1957; Torgerson, 1958). The point representing an item is actually a "cutting point" along the underlying dimension, in the sense that it serves as the boundary between negative and positive responses on the item. In other words, if subjects give negative responses to the item, then their points are located to the left of the cutting point, whereas positive responses correspond to subject points on the right of the cutting point. Dichotomies only have a single cutting point per item, so locating the cutting points seems to be equivalent to locating the items themselves. Polychotomous items simply have more than one cutting point; there is a separate cutting point between each pair of adjacent response categories. If an item has Q categories, then there will be $Q - 1$ cutting points for that item.

In geometric terms, each item is still a replication of the underlying dimension. However, a polychotomy divides the dimension into Q segments, rather than just two segments, as was the case with dichotomous items. A subject's score on an item will automatically pin down that subject's point location relative to all of the item's cutting points; thus it is easy to break each item up into $Q - 1$ dichotomies. The scalogram is then constructed exactly as it was in the case of dichotomous items. The only difference is that the columns of the data matrix now explicitly represent cutting points, rather than the items themselves. If an item has more than two possible responses, it will require more than a single column in the matrix.[10]

The most serious limitation of the traditional Guttman scale approach is that it is based upon a strictly deterministic model. It makes no provisions to explain deviations from perfectly scalable response patterns; it has no theory of scaling errors. Scaling errors occur when a subject gives a negative response to an item with a point that is located to the left of the subject's own point, or when a positive response is given to an item with a point located to the right of the subject's point. In either case, such responses are contradictions, given the geometry of the scaling solution. In the standard Guttman scaling analysis, errors are unexplainable; we merely acknowledge that such responses do exist, and try to develop methods for assigning scale scores to observations that exhibit these kinds of errors. But they remain as gaps in our explanation of the variability in the data.

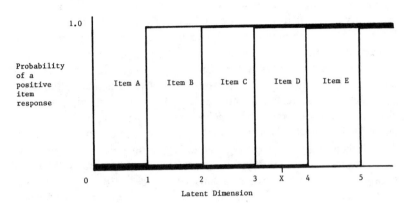

Figure 5.3. Trace Lines for Items in Deterministic Scaling Model

In order to deal with exactly this limitation, probabilistic forms of the cumulative model have been developed. Figures 5.3 and 5.4 show the difference between the deterministic and probabilistic versions of a cumulative scale. The figures give two versions of the trace lines for five items that form a scale. An item's trace lines show the probability of a positive response on that item, at each position along the underlying dimension. Figure 5.3 shows the deterministic model. If a subject's point is located

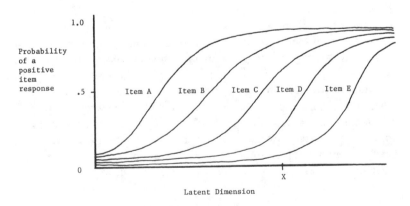

Figure 5.4. Trace Lines for Items in Probabilistic Scaling Model

at a higher position (i.e., farther to the right) than an item point, then the subject *must* give a positive response to that item. There is absolutely no provision for a negative response on an item that falls to the left of the subject point. For example, the point labeled X in Figure 5.3 represents a subject; this person must give a positive response to items A, B, and C because the trace lines for those items show that the probability of a positive response, at the scale position corresponding to X, is identically 1.0 for all three of the items.

But this is too stringent a standard for the real world, precisely because scaling models never fit perfectly. Therefore, the trace lines in Figure 5.4 show a probabilistic version of the same scale. Here, the probability of a positive response for any item increases as one moves to higher positions along the dimension. Thus a subject with a point located at position X in the figure is *likely* to give positive responses to items A, B, and C, and negative responses to items D and E. However, there are still nonzero probabilities of the opposite responses on each of the five items. The varying scale locations of the items are still clearly discernible in the different positions of the separate item trace lines. The cumulative nature of the model is represented by the relations among the probabilities. For any arbitrary subject point along the dimension, the following will always be true:

$$\text{Prob}(A = 1) \geq \text{Prob}(B = 1) \geq \text{Prob}(C = 1) \geq \text{Prob}(D = 1) \geq \text{Prob}(E = 1)$$

Thus the probabilities are:

(1) monotonically related to the position along the underlying dimension; as the item possesses more of the attribute corresponding to the latent dimension, the trace line is shifted to the right (i.e., to a higher numerical position)

(2) monotonically related to each other, at any position along the latent dimension; regardless of the subject's location, a positive response on item A is more likely than a positive response on B, and so on

There are several techniques available for estimating the probabilistic version of the cumulative scale model, including Rasch models (Andrich, 1988), Mokken scales (Mokken, 1970; Mokken and Lewis, 1982; Niemoller and van Schuur, 1983), and latent class models (McCutcheon, 1987). They all represent improvements over the deterministic approach because they explicitly allow for empirical deviations from the "perfect" form of the cumulative scale. Furthermore, they all evaluate the fit of the scaling model against the explicit null hypothesis that the separate item responses are statistically independent of each other. That would be the situation if no latent dimension existed to impose structure on the data. This kind of explicit hypothesis testing is preferable to the ad hoc decisions and rules of thumb (e.g., "the coefficient of reproducibility must be greater than .90") that usually guide judgments about the fit of the cumulative model to a data set.

In strictly practical terms, probabilistic cumulative scaling techniques often lead to the conclusion that a latent dimension exists when the opposite conclusion would have been reached using the traditional Guttman scaling standards. This illustrates the trade-off between the model and the data: As the researcher is willing to make more explicit assumptions about the nature of the errors, it becomes possible to accept greater discrepancies between the perfect scale patterns implied by the scaling model and the empirical data themselves. Thus probabilistic versions of the cumulative scaling model are not only more realistic than the traditional Guttman approach, they also allow scales to be constructed more readily from error-laden data.

Let us next consider the problem of multidimensionality and the cumulative scaling model. Stated simply, the question is, can scaling procedures based upon this model recover the dimensional structure underlying a set of data when the latter are simultaneously affected by *several* independent sources of variability? The general answer to this question is no (Coombs, 1964). The goodness of fit measures used to test the cumulative scaling model can indicate when a single dimension is inadequate to represent the data. However, they cannot be used to discern the reasons that this might occur (i.e., is it lack of structure, measurement error, or a more complicated dimensional structure?). Furthermore, if a unidimensional model is applied to a situation involving multidimensional phenomena, then the scaling technique will usually not successfully estimate *any* of the underlying attributes with any degree of accuracy (Coombs, 1964).[11]

In general, the cumulative scaling approaches work best when applied to data that conform to a unidimensional model in which both sets of objects contained in the data vary systematically according to a single attribute. If the researcher suspects either (1) that only one of the object sets contains systematic variation, or (2) that there are multiple sources of variability in a set of observations, then some other scaling approach would probably prove more useful.

Factor Analysis. Factor analysis is another procedure that can be used to scale single stimulus data. It models responses on a set of empirical items as manifestations of variability along one or more latent dimensions. Thus factor analysis has objectives that are similar to, but more general than, those in summated rating scales and cumulative scales. However, the method employed to estimate the factor analysis model is markedly different from the other two. In this section, we will examine the basic geometry of the factor analysis model. The methods used to estimate this model from empirical data are covered in detail in many sources, including Kim and Mueller (1978a, 1978b) and Long (1983).

As shown in Figure 5.5, factor analysis is applied to an N by K data matrix (usually, observations by variables). The first step of the analysis is usually to obtain correlations between the levels of one mode — usually the variables. These correlations are arranged in a square matrix of order K. The entries in the main diagonal are called *communalities;* they represent the proportion of the total variance in each observed variable that is "explained by" the latent dimensions.[12] The scaling technique decomposes (or "factors") the information in the correlation matrix, to produce a new K by M "factor pattern matrix."[13] This shows the K observed variables' dependencies on M underlying dimensions (which are usually called "factors").[14] The scaling analysis sometimes stops at this point. But, it can proceed by generating an M by K matrix of "factor scoring coefficients." The latter estimate the M latent dimensions as linear functions of the observed variables. The original N by K data matrix can be multiplied by the factor scoring matrix to produce an N by M matrix of "factor scores." These estimate the other mode's (i.e., the observations, if the variables were factored) locations along the underlying factors. In this manner, a factor analysis can be used to scale both sets of points contained in a set of single stimulus data.

The geometric model for factor analysis represents the objects to be scaled (usually, the variables) as vectors within a space formed by the elements in the other mode of the data matrix (an "observation space"). Figure 5.6 shows a simple example of a standard scatter diagram. Here, the axes represent variables (thus, a variable space), and the plotted points represent two observations. Of course, these points are located in the space according to the observations' values on the two variables. Now consider Figure 5.7. Here, the axes and the points are switched. Each observation is an axis, and the plotted points represent the variables. Furthermore, the plotted point is now shown as a vector — a directed line

48

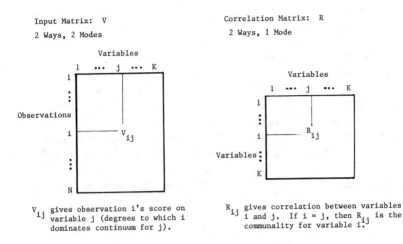

Input Matrix: V
2 Ways, 2 Modes

Variables

1 ··· j ··· K

Observations

V_{ij}

V_{ij} gives observation i's score on variable j (degrees to which i dominates continuum for j).

Correlation Matrix: R
2 Ways, 1 Mode

Variables

1 ··· j ··· K

Variables

R_{ij}

R_{ij} gives correlation between variables i and j. If i = j, then R_{ij} is the communality for variable i.

Scaling Model: Factor pattern coefficients calculated so that scalar products between variable vectors in factor space are as close as possible to correlations. Factor scoring coefficients obtained by regressing factors on empirical variables.

Output Matrices

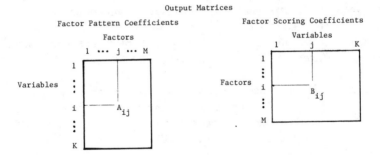

Factor Pattern Coefficients

Factors

1 ··· j ··· M

Variables

A_{ij}

A_{ij} shows impact of factor j on variable i.

Factor Scoring Coefficients

Variables

1 j K

Factors

B_{ij}

B_{ij} shows the "best fitting" coefficient to predict factor i from variable j (and the other empirical variables).

Figure 5.5. Factor Analysis

segment, beginning at the origin of the space and terminating at the plotted point. The locations of the variable vectors are determined by their values on each of the observation-axes.

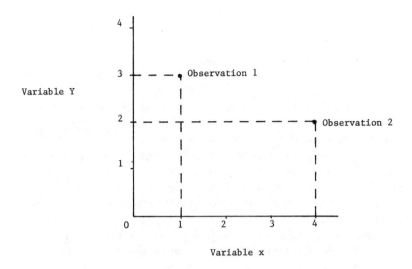

Figure 5.6. Vector Representation of Observation Points in Variable Space

Of course, Figures 5.6 and 5.7 present exactly the same information; they merely show it in different ways. This is an extremely simple

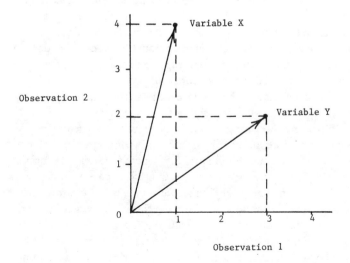

Figure 5.7. Vector Representation of Variable Vectors in Observation Space

example, because there are only two observations. Generally, there should be N perpendicular axes, and each variable vector would have coordinates on each of these axes. Thus the orientation of each vector completely summarizes the information contained in that variable.

When the variable values are expressed as deviations from their respective means, and when each value is divided by the square root of N (the total number of axes in the space), some very useful results occur. First, the variable means are all located at the origin of the space. Second, the squared length of each vector is equal to the variance of the corresponding variable; of course, this also means that the length is the standard deviation. Third, the cosine of the angle between any two vectors is equal to the correlation between those two variables; the smaller the angle, the higher the correlation, and vice versa. A right angle (90 degrees) means that the two variables are uncorrelated (or orthogonal).[15]

Geometrically, the factor analysis begins with K variable vectors located within the N-space formed by the observations. The objective of the scaling technique is to simplify the representation of the variables: Instead of K vectors in an N-space (where N is probably a very large number), we try to locate the K variable vectors within a subspace defined by M new vectors, or "factors" (where M is much smaller than N and, it is hoped, smaller than K). Of course, it will probably be impossible to find a factor subspace that completely contains the variable vectors. This means that the factors cannot account for all of the variance in the observed variables. The factor analysis model handles this by assuming that each observed variable has its own unique component. The component contributes to the variable's variance, but it is entirely separate from (i.e., uncorrelated with) the factors and the other observed variables. This unique component plays a very important role, because it accounts for scaling errors in a factor analysis solution; it explains why the observed variables are not perfectly predictable on the basis of the underlying factors alone.

Figures 5.8 and 5.9 show the geometry of a hypothetical factor analysis solution, involving four observed variables (X_1 through X_4) and two uncorrelated factors (F_1 and F_2). Figure 5.8 shows the subspace formed by the factors.[16] The four vectors shown in this subspace are not the variables themselves. Instead, they are "shadows" of the variables, formed by taking the perpendicular projections from the tips of the respective variable vectors into the factor space. The squared lengths of these shadow vectors are the communalities. The shadow vectors' coordinates on the factor axes show the linear dependencies of the variables on the factors; the larger the value of each coordinate, the stronger the impact of that

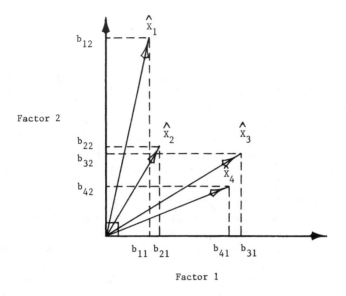

Figure 5.8. Geometric Model for Factor Analysis (Two-Factor Space, Containing Vectors for Empirical Variables — Factors Are Orthogonal)

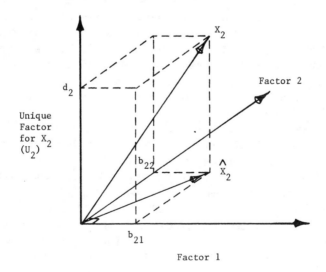

Figure 5.9. Geometric Model for Factor Analysis — Space for Variable X_2

factor on that variable. These coordinates are called *factor pattern co-efficients*. Figure 5.8 shows a plot of the factor pattern for these variables and factors; it contains a great deal of information. Thus we can see that the factors account for twice as much variance in X_1 as X_2, because the X_1 vector is twice as long as that for X_2. At the same time, the second (vertical) factor has a much stronger influence on X_1 than the first factor; the b_{12} coordinate is farther away from the origin (i.e., its numeric value is greater) than the b_{11} coordinate. Figure 5.9 shows the entire vector for variable X_2, and its relation to the factor space. The full vector is contained in a three-dimensional space; two of its dimensions are formed by the F_1, F_2 plane, and the third corresponds to U_2, the unique component for variable X_2. The component's impact on X_2 is measured by the coordinate on the U_2 axis (d_2). In order to graph the X_2 vector completely, we must take all three axes into account; this is the geometric equivalent of saying that the total variance in an observed variable depends upon its unique component, as well as the factors. Figures 5.8 and 5.9 clearly show that the observed variables' dependencies on the factors are modeled by the orientations of the variable vectors relative to the factor axes; the closer the former comes to the latter, the stronger the impact of the factors on the variables.

But how do we determine the subspace containing the factor axes relative to the variable vectors? The factor subspace is located by using the following criterion: The scalar products between each pair of shadow vectors should come as close as possible to the observed correlations between the respective pairs of variables.[17] Ideally, the scalar products should equal the correlations. In this sense, the factor space explains the correlations between the empirical variables. And it divides the total observed variance in each variable into two parts: (a) The communality, which lies in the factor space and is therefore shared with the other variables; and (b) the uniqueness, which is outside of and uncorrelated with the factor space — therefore, it is the part of the variable's variance that is not shared with any other variables (observed or unobserved).

The scalar product criterion for fitting the factor model leads to some of the troublesome indeterminacies involved in this model. The scalar product of two vectors depends entirely upon the orientation of those vectors relative to each other, and *not* upon the vectors' locations relative to the axes of the space. This means that for any arbitrary number of factors there is an infinite number of factor solutions, corresponding to all of the possible orientations of the factor axes relative to the shadow vectors (i.e., the rotation problem). Similarly, the factor axes may be at right angles to each other (i.e., an orthogonal factor solution), or they may form some other angles (an oblique solution). Once again, the scalar products between the variables' shadow vectors will remain unchanged.

Factor analysis can be used to determine whether K variables and N observations can be modeled as points in *some* M-dimensional factor space. However, the exact nature of this space must be discerned on the basis of criteria that are essentially separate from the factor analysis itself (e.g., simple structure guidelines for rotation, and substantive theory for correlated versus uncorrelated factors). This inability to use an "objective procedure" to pin down a precise scaling solution is often very frustrating (Steiger and Schonemann, 1978). However, the problem is inescapable, and it should not cause potential users to overlook a research tool that can be very useful: Factor analysis still provides useful insights into the common sources of variability underlying objects.

Stimulus Comparison Data

Stimulus comparison data are relatively uncommon in nonexperimental settings.[18] And when they do arise, stimulus comparisons are often uninteresting for scaling purposes. After all, if the objects are compared to each other using a common standard, then the very existence of the standard implies that the objects can be located along a dimension. As a result, further measurement or scaling operations may be unnecessary. It is only when the stimulus comparisons fail to provide enough information in themselves that scaling methods must be employed. Although there are a few methods for analyzing stimulus comparison data, they are among the least-used scaling models considered in this chapter.

Scaling Methods for Stimulus Comparison Data. The method of paired comparisons, initially developed by L. L. Thurstone, uses a scaling model that is appropriate for stimulus comparisons (e.g., Edwards, 1957). The model assumes that the stimulus objects are represented as probability distributions, rather than fixed points, along the latent dimension. When one object is compared to another, single points are sampled from each of their distributions. The point estimate for each object corresponds to the mean of that object's distribution. Thurstone's contribution was a method for estimating the relative locations of the stimulus means, using the observed probabilities of one stimulus dominating another.

54

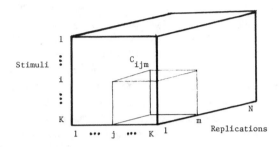

C_{ijm} is "1" if stimulus i dominates stimulus j on replication m, "0" if j dominates i on that replication.

Figure 5.10. Paired Comparisons Scale (Input Matrix)

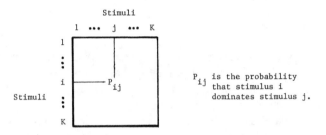

P_{ij} is the probability that stimulus i dominates stimulus j.

Scaling Model: Distance between stimulus points i and j are a function of probability, P_{ij}.

Figure 5.11. Paired Comparisons Scale (Probability Matrix)

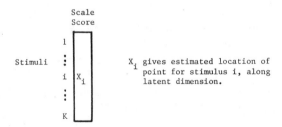

X_i gives estimated location of point for stimulus i, along latent dimension.

Figure 5.12. Paired Comparisons Scale (Output Matrix)

The method of paired comparisons begins with a three-way, two-mode matrix of dichotomous data, as shown in Figure 5.10. The first two ways correspond to the K stimuli, so there are K levels in each way. The cell entries show whether the row stimulus dominates the column stimulus, or vice versa. The third way, and second mode, consists of N replications for each pair of stimuli. In many applications, the stimuli pairs correspond to N subjects. The scaling technique begins by collapsing the data matrix across the levels of the third way, resulting in the two-way, single-mode matrix shown in Figure 5.11. Now, the cell entries are interpreted as the probabilities that the row stimuli dominate the column stimuli. Thurstone's method is applied directly to this matrix of probabilities to produce a square matrix of estimated distances between the K stimulus points (which are, themselves, the means of the distributions). Finally, one stimulus is arbitrarily placed at the origin of the dimension, and the scale values of the remaining stimuli are calculated according to their distances from this stimulus; this produces the K by 1 vector of scale scores shown in Figure 5.12. The resultant scale is related to the probabilities, usually by the inverse of the normal density function (i.e., Z-scores are obtained by "working backwards" from the probabilities). The fact that there is a specific relationship between observations and scores, along with the arbitrary location of the origin, means that the paired comparison method produces interval level measurement.

Psychophysical magnitude scaling is another approach that can be used for stimulus comparison data. This model is based upon Steven's (1957) law of ratio estimation; specific scaling techniques based upon this model are covered by Lodge (1981). Ideally, the data for a psychophysical magnitude scaling analysis would consist of *two separate* three-way, three-mode matrices; the first matrix would contain observations on a set of calibration stimuli, whereas the second matrix would contain the observations pertaining to the substantive stimulus objects. The interpretation of the two matrices is essentially identical (see Figure 5.13). The first way and mode of the matrix contains two levels, corresponding to the two separate response modalities. The second way and mode contains K levels, one for each stimulus. The third way and mode corresponds to replications of the magnitude judgments; there are N levels in this way, often corresponding to separate subjects. The cell entries in the data matrix contain judgments about the relative magnitudes of two stimuli: The magnitude of the column stimulus is expressed as a ratio of the magnitude of a reference stimulus. For each of the K stimuli, the

56

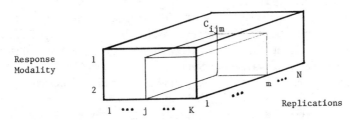

C_{ijm} is the ratio of stimulus j's magnitude to the magnitude of the reference stimulus, measured according to response modality l, on replication m.

Scaling Model: Stimulus points are located along dimension by raising each C_{ijk} to power given by characteristic exponent for response modality i. Input matrix is collapsed by taking geometric means across modes for replications and response modalities.

Output Matrix: X

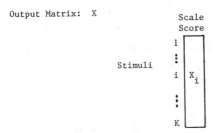

X_i gives location of point for stimulus i, based upon ratio comparison to a specified reference stimulus.

*There would be two separate input matrices-- one for calibration stimuli and one for the substantive stimuli. Both input matrices would be the same shape.

Figure 5.13. Psychophysical Magnitude Scale

magnitude judgment is repeated once for each response modality and for each replication.

In data theory terms, the magnitude judgments express the degree to which one stimulus dominates another (i.e., the reference stimulus). Geometrically, the stimuli are modeled as points along a latent dimension corresponding to the specified attribute (i.e., the basis for the magnitude judgments). The stimuli are located by arbitrarily fixing the point for the reference stimulus; the values for the remaining stimulus points are determined by their ratios to the reference stimulus. The scale values are related to the magnitude judgments by a specific power function (which is, itself, determined by the characteristic exponents for the response modalities). Furthermore, the use of ratio judgments implies that the origin of the dimension is fixed. Therefore, psychophysical magnitude scales are believed to provide ratio level measurement of underlying stimulus characteristics.

Assessment of Scaling Methods for Stimulus Comparisons. In substantive and practical terms, the empirical observations required to perform a psychophysical magnitude scaling analysis are very different from those required for the method of paired comparisons. However, from a data theory perspective, the differences between them are quite simple: With paired comparisons, we need dominance relations between every pair of stimuli. In magnitude scaling, each stimulus is compared only against a single reference stimulus. Apart from this, the two scaling models proceed in a similar manner, using dominance relations between pairs of stimuli to provide information about the relative locations of points along a dimension.

These two stimulus comparison methods are very powerful scaling techniques. However, they do have at least two problems that may limit their usefulness in certain situations. The first concerns the dimensionality of the attribute being measured. Both methods require the analyst to specify the *nature* of the dimension in advance; in other words, one stimulus is compared to another on the basis of a clearly defined characteristic. This can be a weakness if the researcher is uncertain about the existence or nature of the substantive property itself. In the most extreme case, the researcher might specify a criterion for the comparisons with which the subjects are completely unfamiliar. Any scaling results from such an analysis would be meaningless. This problem would probably be manifested as a poor fit between the scale and the data, but the source of the problem would not be clear: It could be the wrong specification, a lack of structure, or a multidimensional structure within the data. Thus these methods are problematic when applied as scaling criteria.

The second problem is more practical in nature. Stimulus comparison methods tend to be heavily data intensive. In other words, they require a great deal of empirical information before it is possible to estimate the stimulus locations along the latent dimension. Data collection is always costly, and researchers must consider whether these costs can justify the benefits that the empirical scales may provide. In many situations, it may simply be more efficient to obtain different data and use other scaling methods. This seems to be the main reason for the infrequency of paired comparison analyses, and it surely inhibits the wider application of psychophysical magnitude scaling techniques as well.

Similarities Data

Similarities data are usually used for multidimensional scaling (MDS). In an MDS analysis, the entries in the data matrix are modeled as distances between points in a space (e.g., Arabie, Carroll, and DeSarbo, 1987; Kruskal and Wish, 1978). The greater the proximity (or "similarity") between two objects, the *smaller* the distance between their points. In order to avoid this inverse relation between the data values and the geometric model, it is common to reverse the entries in the data matrix, changing similarities into *dissimilarities*.[19] After such a transformation is carried out, the numerical magnitudes of the data values are directly related to interpoint distances in the scaled space (larger values correspond to larger distances). Reversing the data values causes no problems, because the transformation preserves all of the information contained in the original data matrix.

Different Variations of MDS. There are many different varieties of MDS (e.g., Young, 1987). From a data theory perspective, their differences involve the interpretation of the entries in the data matrix, as well as the shape of the data matrix itself. Perhaps the most fundamental difference involves the distinction between metric and nonmetric MDS analyses. Stated simply, a metric analysis assumes that the input data are measured at the interval or ratio level, whereas a nonmetric analysis permits ordinal and even nominal data. In a metric MDS, the data values are transformed into interpoint distances according to a specific function (e.g., distances may be linearly related to dissimilarities); in a nonmetric MDS, the transformation from data to model can follow any monotonic form, so long as increasing dissimilarity does not correspond to *decreasing* distances. Note that the metric-nonmetric distinction applies *only* to the input data. Both forms of MDS produce a metric model in their output:

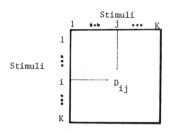

Figure 5.14. Multidimensional Scaling of Two-Way Matrix (Input Matrix — 2 Ways, 1 Mode)

The distances between the object points are ratio level, whereas the object coordinates in the space are interval level.

The simplest data matrix for an MDS analysis has two ways and one mode, as shown in Figure 5.14. The single mode has K levels, corresponding to the stimulus objects. Each cell entry measures the dissimilarity between the objects represented in that row and that column. The matrix may or may not be symmetric about its main diagonal. If the entries are symmetric (that is, the dissimilarity between objects A and B equals the dissimilarity between B and A), then the data can be transformed directly into distances (which are, by definition, symmetric). Figure 5.15 shows the results from an MDS analysis of a two-way, one-mode symmetric matrix of dissimilarities data. The output matrix is K by M, given the coordinates of the K stimulus points along the M axes in the space. Of course, the coordinates can be used to recover the interpoint distances, using the familiar Euclidean distance formula. This is the simplest variation; it is sometimes called *classical multidimensional scaling* or CMDS.

What if the entries in the data matrix are asymmetric, so that the dissimilarity between A and B is *not* equal to that between B and A? The course of action depends entirely upon the researcher's interpretation of the asymmetry. In many cases, the asymmetry is *substantively* uninteresting. For example, it may simply represent measurement error, or fluctuations in judgments. In that case, the asymmetry would not be a part of the geometric model used to represent the data. Any empirical asymmetries would be eliminated *before* the scaling analysis actually began, perhaps by taking the mean of the entries above and below the main diagonal of the matrix. The result would be a symmetric dissimilarities

60

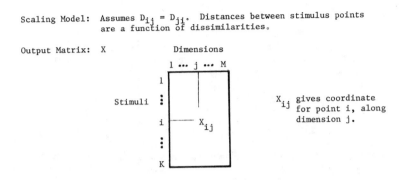

Figure 5.15. Multidimensional Scaling of Two-Way Matrix (Classical MDS)

matrix, and the rest of the analysis would proceed as a CMDS. On the other hand, the asymmetries may, in fact, be substantively interesting. For example, there may be some kind of order effects, in which the nature of the first stimulus affects the response to the second stimulus. In that case, the researcher probably would want to include them in the geometric model produced by the scaling analysis; this would be an *asymmetric multidimensional scaling analysis* (or AMDS). One way of doing so is to analyze the data using Young's ASYMSCAL model.[20] This produces results that are diagrammed in Figure 5.16. There is still a K by M matrix of stimulus point coordinates. But now, there is also a K by M matrix of stimulus weights. When calculating the distance from, say, A to B, A's weights are used to distort the differences between A and B, along each of the M dimensions. Because the weights for A can be different from the weights for B, the overall distances can be asymmetric. Although this example shows the flexibility of the MDS approach, it should be noted that there are very few substantive applications of the ASYMSCAL model.

Figure 5.17 shows a three-way, two-mode matrix of dissimilarities. The first two ways and the first mode are all identical to the previous situation. The third way (which is also the second mode) consists of repeated observations on the dissimilarities. Thus each entry in this matrix (say, d_{ijn}) represents the dissimilarity between stimulus i and stimulus j, as measured by data source n.

How are the objects in the third way (and second mode) incorporated into the scaling analysis? Once again, this depends entirely upon the

Scaling Model: Assumes $D_{ij} \neq D_{ji}$. Distances between stimuli are a function of dissimilarities. Each stimulus also has an idiosyncratic weight for each of the dimensions.

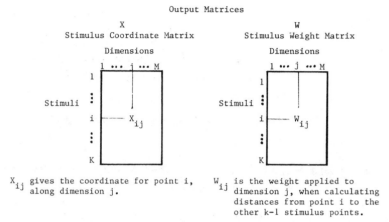

Output Matrices

X
Stimulus Coordinate Matrix

W
Stimulus Weight Matrix

X_{ij} gives the coordinate for point i, along dimension j.

W_{ij} is the weight applied to dimension j, when calculating distances from point i to the other k-1 stimulus points.

Figure 5.16. Multidimensional Scaling of Two-Way Matrix (Assymetric MDS)

researcher's interpretation of the information supplied by these objects. The differences across the data sources may not be substantively interesting; the third way would then be treated as simple replications of the original dissimilarities among the *K* stimuli. For example, there may be similarity judgments given by *N* judges, drawn from a homogeneous population. In that case, a *replicated MDS* or RMDS analysis could be

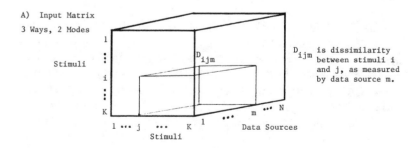

A) Input Matrix
3 Ways, 2 Modes

D_{ijm} is dissimilarity between stimuli i and j, as measured by data source m.

Figure 5.17. Multidimensional Scaling of Two-Way Matrix (Input Matrix — 3 Ways, 2 Modes)

62

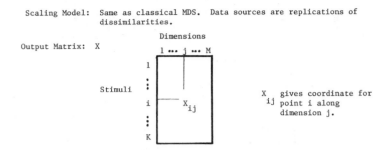

Figure 5.18. Multidimensional Scaling of Two-Way Matrix (Replicated MDS)

used to collapse across the third way of the matrix, producing the standard *K* by *M* matrix of stimulus point coordinates shown in Figure 5.18. The practical advantage of RMDS is that we presumably have more reliable estimates of the dissimilarities between the stimuli.

If the *N* data sources do vary in substantively interesting ways, then the researcher would want to incorporate these differences into the geometric model. The most common strategy for doing so is *weighted multidimensional scaling* or WMDS (Arabie, Carroll, and DeSarbo, 1987). There are several different forms of WMDS, but they all produce the kind of information shown in Figure 5.19. As usual, there is a *K* by *M* matrix of stimulus coordinates. But now, there is also a separate *M* by *M* weight matrix for each of the *N* data sources; this is shown as a single *M* by *M* by *N* matrix in the figure. The nature of the geometric model is determined by the contents of the weight matrices. If they are all identity matrices, then the results reduce to the RMDS model. If all of the weight matrices only have nonzero entries in their main diagonals, then the result is the familiar INDSCAL model (Carroll and Chang, 1970); for each data source, the interpoint differences along each axis are stretched or shrunk according to the values of the weights. If the weight matrices are symmetric, then the result is the IDIOSCAL (Carroll and Chang, 1970) or GEMSCAL model (Young, 1987); each data source corresponds to a different rotation of the stimulus space, along with the differential stretching and shrinking of each dimension.[21] These variations do not exhaust the possibilities, by any means. However, the INDSCAL model is really the only version of WMDS that has received widespread use in substantive analyses.

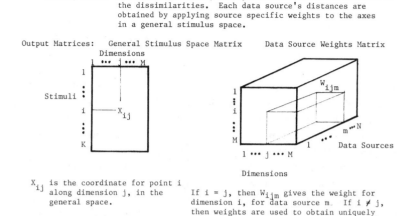

Scaling Model: For each data source, interpoint distances are a function of the dissimilarities. Each data source's distances are obtained by applying source specific weights to the axes in a general stimulus space.

X_{ij} is the coordinate for point i along dimension j, in the general space.

If $i = j$, then W_{ijm} gives the weight for dimension i, for data source m. If $i \neq j$, then weights are used to obtain uniquely rotated axes for data source m.

Figure 5.19. Multidimensional Scaling of Two-Way Matrix (Weighted MDS)

Multidimensional Scaling and Factor Analysis. There are some important parallels between MDS and factor analysis. Both scaling strategies use a two-way, one-mode data matrix (dissimilarities for MDS and correlations for factor analysis) in order to generate a multidimensional configuration of object points. Indeed, the correlation matrix is often interpreted as a matrix of proximities (even though it is constructed from single stimulus data). What, then, distinguishes between factor analysis and MDS? Why use one technique rather than the other? The fundamental difference between them lies in the ways they model the entries in their respective data matrices. Factor analysis represents correlations as *scalar products*; the latter are functions of vector lengths (i.e., the communalities) and the angles between the vectors. MDS models dissimilarities as *distances*. Thus the two scaling strategies differ in the kind of "geometric picture" they construct for the input data. All of the other differences between them are subordinate to this fundamental distinction.[22]

A researcher's decision to use factor analysis or MDS should be based entirely upon the most reasonable interpretation of the data. If the entries in the data matrix are best represented as scalar products, then factor analysis should be used; if the data can be accurately modeled as distances, then MDS is appropriate. Correlation coefficients (and directly related measures like covariances) are about the only kind of data that are routinely interpreted as scalar products. In contrast, there are many kinds of empirical observations that could be interpreted as similarities data. These include: direct similarity judgments; physical distances; joint probabilities (i.e., how frequently two events occur together); and conditional probabilities (i.e., given that one event has occurred, how frequently does the other occur?). Useful and detailed discussion of such measures are included in a variety of sources, including Schiffman, Reynolds, and Young (1981), Coxon (1982), and Davison (1983), as well as the volume by Kruskal and Wish (1978) in this monograph series.

It is important to emphasize that correlation coefficients *do not* work very well when they are interpreted as similarities data. Figure 5.20 shows vectors representing three variables: *A, B,* and *C.* Assume that we have correlations between these variables. An MDS analysis would use the input data to estimate the distances between the three terminal points of the vectors. From the figure, it is easy to see that these distances are ordered as follows: $d_{AC} < d_{AB} < d_{BC}$. Of course, these distances are not known a priori; the only information the researcher possesses is the set of correlations. But these values correspond to the *cosines* of the angles between the vectors. Obviously, there is a problem: The highest correlation (which MDS would model as the smallest distance) is between A and B; the second highest is between B and C; the smallest correlation (modeled as the largest distance) is that between A and C. Thus the correlations would seriously distort the distances between the points. This simple example shows that correlations *cannot* be modeled accurately as distances; therefore, they should not generally be used as input data for an MDS analysis.[23] Instead, factor analysis is the preferred method for analyzing a matrix of correlation coefficients.

Profile Distances. As an alternative to correlations, profile distances are sometimes used to convert single stimulus data into similarities. Assume that we want to perform an MDS analysis on a set of objects, using data in a K by Q, objects by variables matrix. The Euclidean distance formula can be used to calculate dissimilarities between objects by taking the square root of the sum of square differences, across the variables, for every pair of observations in the data matrix.[24] The resultant values (one value for each pair of observations) are, in fact, distances between the objects in a Q-dimensional variable space. MDS can be used to recover these distances.

An MDS analysis based upon profile distances can be used to reduce the sheer amount of data facing the researcher. But in many cases, the

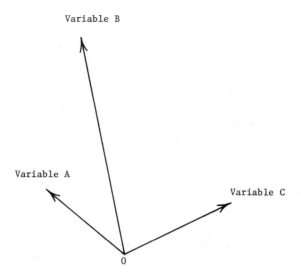

True Distances:

    Dist (A,C)* $<$ Dist (A,B) $<$ Dist (B,C)

    $\angle$ AOB = 39 degrees, COS $\angle$ AOB = r_{AB} = .78

    $\angle$ AOC = 116 degrees, COS $\angle$ AOC = r_{AC} = -.44

    $\angle$ BOC = 77 degrees, COS $\angle$ BOC = r_{BC} = .22

Incorrect Distances, estimated from correlations:

    Dist (A,B) $<$ Dist (B,C) $<$ Dist (A,C)

*Dist (A,C) means "the distance between the A point and the C point."

Figure 5.20. Variable Vectors, Correlations, and Interpoint Distances

main objective of the analysis is to discern the underlying structure among a set of objects, without imposing the researcher's own ideas about how the objects differ among themselves. Profile distance data are much *less* useful for this purpose, because the researcher has decided on the variables that will go into the profile. In doing so, it is easy to influence the nature of the dimensions that will be obtained from the analysis. The dimensions of the space in the scaling result will tend to correspond to the variables with the largest variances — that is, the variables that exhibit the largest differences in their values across the objects. And, of course, these variables are selected by the researcher in the first place. Thus profile distances can be used to *summarize* a great deal of information succinctly about the objects under investigation. However, they are much less likely to produce new insights about the *sources* of variability among the objects.

Preferential Choice Data

Preferential choice data are usually analyzed with the unfolding model (e.g., Coombs, 1964; McIver and Carmines, 1981). As shown in Figure 5.21, the simplest data matrix would contain two ways and two modes; the modes are often called "subjects" and "stimuli," although they could easily correspond to other types of objects. The cell entries measure the proximities between the respective row and column objects. An unfolding analysis produces two separate matrices: The first matrix give the coordinates for a set of points representing the subjects. The second matrix gives the coordinates for points representing the stimuli. Both of these point sets are contained in the same "joint space." The subject and stimulus points are located relative to each other, according to the following rule: The greater the preference of subject i for stimulus j, the smaller the distance between the point representing i and the point representing j.[25] There are many different procedures for fitting the unfolding model to empirical preferential choice data, and the variety among them is far too great to be covered in the monograph. Thompson (1988) provides a brief but comprehensive review of the different approaches to unfolding.

Problems in Multidimensional Unfolding. The unfolding model focuses entirely on representing proximity information in the data as distances within a space; this model transcends the dimensionality of the space itself. If subjects use a single criterion to judge the stimuli, then a single dimension is appropriate to array the subject and stimulus points. If subjects use several criteria simultaneously to form their judgments, then a multidimensional space will be needed to locate the subject and stimulus points.

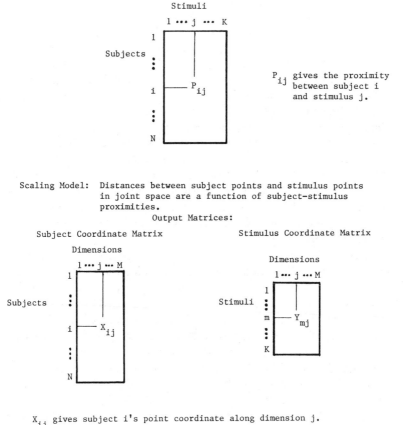

P_{ij} gives the proximity between subject i and stimulus j.

Scaling Model: Distances between subject points and stimulus points in joint space are a function of subject-stimulus proximities.

Output Matrices:

X_{ij} gives subject i's point coordinate along dimension j.

Y_{mj} gives stimulus m's point coordinate along dimension j.

Figure 5.21. Unfolding Analysis

Even though the multidimensional unfolding *model* is well developed, virtually all of the algorithms for fitting this model to data are problematic. The difficulty arises because there is a relatively small amount of empirical data (the *N* by *K* data matrix) used to estimate a fairly large amount of information (the *N* by *M* matrix of subject point coordinates, along with the *K* by *M* matrix of stimulus point coordinates). As a result, there are often many different point configurations that can provide an equally acceptable fit to the data. Therefore, an estimated multidimensional joint space can only be regarded with caution. In extreme situations, degenerate scaling solutions can result, in which all of the objects in one of the data modes are located at a single point in the space. The only solution to this problem is to increase the amount of data relative to the number of points. One approach is to obtain replicated preferential choice data; algorithms based upon this approach seem to work quite well (e.g., DeSarbo and Carroll, 1985). But replicated data are often unavailable, especially in nonexperimental situations.

An alternative approach is to perform an *external* unfolding analysis. This assumes that one of the point configurations is already known (obtained from prior information of some kind), and the other set of points is unfolded "into" the space that already contains the first set of points (Carroll, 1972). This is a much more tractable problem, because there are far fewer point coordinates that need to be estimated, relative to the amount of input data.[26]

Of course, the external unfolding approach still begs the question of the first point configuration. The obvious solution is to have coordinates for the stimuli obtained from a previous MDS analysis that used suitable similarities data for the stimuli. This could be obtained from information that is completely separate from the data used in the external unfolding analysis. Or, there are at least two methods of using the preference data themselves in order to obtain the similarities data.

First, Rabinowitz (1976) developed the "line-of-sight" measure (LOS) for exactly this purpose. The basic idea behind this method is shown in Figure 5.22. The figure depicts a simple space, containing two stimulus points (A and B) and four subjects' ideal points (W, X, Y, and Z). Assume that the values of the preference data are exactly equal to the distances between the ideal points and the stimulus points; this means that the data have been preprocessed so that *decreasing* distances correspond to *increasing* preferences. For each subject, we can sum the preference values across the two stimuli (that is, simply add W's preference value for A to W's preference value for B, and do the same thing for the other three subjects). Similarly, we can take the difference between the two preference values given by each subject. Visual inspection of the figure will verify that the distance between A and B is measured by the *smallest sum* and also by the *largest difference*. Thus the summed preference values for subject W and the absolute difference of the preference values for subject Z both measure the distance between A and B. This result occurs because the points for W and Z lie precisely on the line connecting A and B. Of

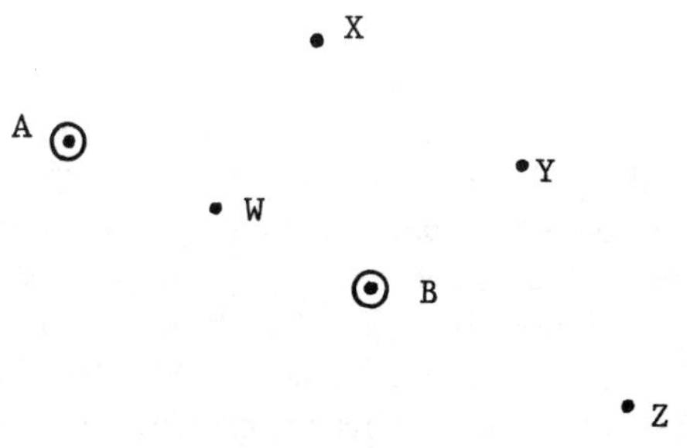

Dist (A,B) = 35

P:

Stimuli

	A	B
W	16	19
X	29	26
Y	50	20
Z	65	30

Subjects

	Sums $(P_A + P_B)$	Differences $(|P_A - P_B|)$
W	35*	3
X	55	3
Y	70	30
Z	95	35**

*Smallest sum

**Largest difference

Figure 5.22. The Line-of-Sight Approach for Obtaining Similarities Data From Preferences

course, none of these point locations are known beforehand. Rabinowitz (1976) showed that, given certain assumptions about the distribution of the points, the *rank-order* of the distances between pairs of stimuli can be obtained by taking the smallest sums and the largest differences of the preference ratings for each pair of stimuli (even though none of the subject points may lie on the line connecting a pair of stimulus points). The actual method is a bit more complex, but this brief description should give the basic idea. The LOS measure is calculated for the stimuli, used as input to an MDS algorithm, and the results provide the stimulus configuration for the external unfolding analysis.

Rodgers and Young (1981) suggest another strategy, called "successive unfolding." This approach proceeds in two steps. First, the N subjects' preference data values for each stimulus are interpreted as a profile for that stimulus; they are used to calculate profile distance measures for every pair of stimuli. This aggregates the preference data across the rows of the original data matrix, producing a matrix of similarities data, which is input to an MDS routine. The MDS routine provides a stimulus configuration, and the preference data are used a second time to locate the subject points relative to the stimulus points.

Dichotomous Preferential Choice Data. Recall from the discussion in Chapter 3 that it is possible to have dichotomous preferential choice data. Such data can be analyzed by a variant of the unfolding model, which is sometimes called "proximity scaling" (e.g., Coombs, 1964; Coombs and Smith, 1973; Weisberg, 1972, 1974). Figures 5.23, 5.24, and 5.25 show a simple example of a proximity scale. The top part of the figure depicts a two-way, two-mode matrix of dichotomous data. Assume that the rows are subjects, the columns are stimuli, and that the cell entries indicate whether the subject *chooses* the stimulus (1) or fails to choose the stimulus (0). Consistent with the unfolding model, we assume that subjects choose the most proximal stimuli to themselves. If this is the case, and if choices are based upon a single, common criterion (i.e., they are unidimensional), then it should be possible to permute the columns of the data matrix to obtain a solid band of 1s in each row; the width of the band varies, because subjects can choose as many stimuli as they want. This is carried out in Figure 5.24. The order of the stimuli along the dimension is given by the order of the columns in the matrix. Geometrically, this corresponds to the ordering of the stimulus points along the latent dimension (Figure 5.25). It is as if each ideal point is surrounded by "boundaries of acceptance." If a stimulus point falls within these boundaries, then it is chosen by that

Stimuli

	A	B	C	D
1	1	1	0	1
2	0	0	1	1
3	1	1	1	1
4	1	1	0	0
5	1	0	1	1
6	1	0	0	1

Subjects

Figure 5.23. Hypothetical Proximity Scale Analysis (Input Matrix)

Stimuli

	C	D	A	B
1	0	1	1	1
2	1	1	0	0
3	1	1	1	1
4	0	0	1	1
5	1	1	1	0
6	0	1	1	0

Subjects

Figure 5.24. Hypothetical Proximity Scale Analysis (Scaling Model — Rearranged Matrix

C	1*
D	2
A	3
B	4

*Entries give rank order
of stimulus points along
the latent dimension.

Figure 5.25. Hypothetical Proximity Scale Analysis (Output Matrix)

subject; otherwise it is not chosen. Note that the ideal points are not located very precisely with this model, because we can only pin them down to their respective sets of chosen stimuli.[27]

There are several possible ways to fit the proximity model to empirical data. The most obvious is simply to permute the rows and columns of the data matrix by hand until the best-fitting pattern is found. This is often not too difficult, if the number of stimuli and distinct response profiles are both relatively small. Alternatively, computer software for unfolding analysis (e.g., ALSCAL) usually permits the use of dichotomous data as input. Finally, the MUDFOLD (*m*ultiple *uni*dimensional un*fold*ing) approach (van Schuur, 1984) was designed specifically for this purpose.[28] Dichotomous preferential choice data are fairly common. Therefore, these scaling approaches can be very useful. These give researchers a powerful model for analyzing the structure contained within behavior that is qualitative in nature.

Interpretations of Data

There is never any single correct type of data that must be extracted from a given set of empirical observations. The interpretation of the data is always based on a combination of substantive considerations (which interpretation of the observations makes the most sense?) and analytic objectives (which scaling procedure will produce the kind of information desired?). To illustrate how the researcher takes an active part in interpreting empirical observations, consider a simple example: A set of N students, each of whom gives a response on K different test questions. The entries in the resultant data matrix are dichotomous (0 for incorrect, and 1 for correct responses).

How should these observations be interpreted? The answer depends on a number of factors. From one perspective, the responses could be single stimulus data (a correct answer means that the student's ability dominates the difficulty level of the test item, and vice versa). From another perspective, the responses could be dichotomous preferential choice data (a correct response means that the student's skills are proximal to those required to answer the question successfully).

For the moment, we will accept the single stimulus interpretation (as most teachers do when they test their students). This narrows down the range of possible scaling strategies, but we still need to decide how to interpret the two elements of each observation. The students are fairly straightforward — we want to represent them as points along a dimension, arrayed according to their test performance. Performance is measured by the number of correct answers; the more correct answers given by a student, the greater the extent to which that student's point dominates the item points, and hence it is located at a numerically higher position along the continuum. But what about the test items? Are these items equally good measures of the skills that are being tested, so that they only differ randomly among themselves? If so (or if we are simply uninterested in variability across items), we can use a scaling procedure that only locates the student points on the dimension (i.e., a summated rating scale); thus, students' test scores are simply based on the summed number of 1s in each row of the data matrix. On the other hand, the differences across the items may be substantively interesting (e.g., in the development of a battery of standard items that can be used for future testing purposes). In that case, we would want to use a method that simultaneously locates points for the items as well as the stimuli (e.g., a cumulative scale).

Further decisions must be made if the data do not meet the scaling criterion for the method that is chosen — in other words, if the empirical responses are not consistent with a single dimension. One possibility would be to move to a less stringent scaling model; that is, one that includes a wider variety of response patterns in its definition of "structure within the data." Thus, if the data do not fit a cumulative scale, we could try a summated rating scale (thereby implicitly concluding that the test items do not, in fact, vary systematically among themselves, even though the students may still do so). Or, if the summated rating model does not fit (i.e., the reliability is too low), then we could try the unfolding model (which incorporates a wider variety of response patterns as perfectly scalable observations). Of course, in doing the latter, we are implicitly giving up on the objective of *ranking* the students according to their respective skill levels; the proximity model admits that students may possess different combinations of skills (gauged by which items they answer correctly), but it makes it more difficult to say that some students possess *more* of the underlying trait than other students.

Of course, we could continue on with this example. But the overall point of the discussion is probably already clear. The nature of data is never predetermined. Instead, the data depend upon the researcher's *interpretation* of the observations. Differing interpretations lead to the application of different scaling procedures which, in turn, directly affect the kind of information that is extracted from the analysis. The researcher must decide which interpretation is most appropriate, and work accordingly. This is an important *creative* component of empirical research in the social sciences.

6. ALTERNATING LEAST SQUARES, OPTIMAL SCALING

Statistical models provide formal representations of observations, *given* a particular set of data values. Traditional approaches to statistical analysis take the numbers assigned to the observations as a fixed set of assumptions that cannot be altered during the course of the analysis. But this rigid interpretation of the numeric values ignores the fact that measurement is, itself, an abstract model for a set of observations. As explained back in Chapter 2, the measurement characteristics of the data can also be regarded as parameters to be estimated during the course of an analysis. The Alternating Least Squares, Optimal Scaling (ALSOS) approach to data analysis is based upon exactly this idea. The ALSOS approach holds that empirical statistical analyses involve two different models of the observations. The first represents the structural relationships between the variables. The second involves the measurement characteristics of the variables. The parameters of *both* models are estimated during the course of an ALSOS analysis.

The difference between standard statistical methods and the ALSOS approach is probably most evident in the ways they deal with variables that are measured at the nominal and ordinal levels. Traditionally, these "lower" levels of measurement have been regarded as problematic barriers to the use of powerful statistical techniques. The ALSOS strategy takes exactly the opposite view: Lower measurement levels provide greater flexibility, which can be exploited in order to maximize the fit between a model and a set of empirical observations.

ALSOS is not a particular technique, or specific model. Instead, it is a general approach to data analysis (Young, 1981).[29] In this discussion, we will focus on the ALSOS version of multiple regression, in which a single dependent variable is expressed as a linear function of several independent variables (Young, de Leeuw, and Takane, 1976). However, it is important to keep in mind that the same strategy could be used with any other statistical procedure (e.g., ANOVA, principal components, or discriminant analysis). In fact, we will see that one of the major strengths of ALSOS is its generality, and broad applicability, under a wide variety of situations.

The ALSOS regression approach is similar to any other least squares method in that it provides the "best-fitting" parameter estimates for a given data set. But the ALSOS strategy differs from others in that it estimates *two* distinct sets of parameters. First, there are the *model* parameters — the regression coefficients. As usual, these are calculated in order to minimize the sum of squared residuals (or maximize the R^2). At this point, ALSOS and the traditional procedures diverge. Most statistical approaches view the data values as fixed, so the estimation would be completed after the first set of parameters. However, ALSOS proceeds to a second step, the estimation of a set of *measurement* parameters. Here, the ALSOS routine seeks a set of specific data values that simultaneously maximize the R^2 and retain the prespecified measurement characteristics for each variable; in this sense, these measurement parameter estimates are the *optimally scaled* values for the observations. The end result of an ALSOS analysis is an estimated statistical model that provides the best fit to the data in terms of *both* the coefficients and the data values. Thus the ALSOS approach gives a very reasonable solution to the problem of regression with qualitative variables. Nominal and ordinal variables would simply be assigned values that result in the highest possible R^2 and still maintain either the categories (for nominal variables) or the ordering (for ordinal variables) of the original observation categories.

The full ALSOS regression algorithm is a bit more complex, but not by much. We begin with two matrices of empirical observations that, together, comprise the initial data:

Y = An N by 1 vector of dependent variable values.

X = An N by $K + 1$ matrix of independent variable values. X can be viewed as a partitioned matrix of column vectors: $[X_0 X_1 X_2 \ldots X_j \ldots X_K]$. The X_0 vector is a unit vector, included to give the model an intercept.

Note that the measurement characteristics must be specified a priori; they can differ across the variables. Some of the Y or X_j might be interval level, others ordinal, and still others can be nominal categories. Further, some variables might be continuous, capable of taking on any values across their ranges; others can be discrete with only a limited number of distinct values.

ALSOS regression estimates the parameters in the following equation:

$$Y^* = X^*\beta^* + E^* \qquad [6.1]$$

$$\text{Where} \quad Y^* = f(Y) \qquad [6.2]$$

$$X^* = [f(X_0)\, f(X_1)\, f(X_2) \ldots f(X_k)] \qquad [6.3]$$

$$\beta^* = (X^{*\prime}X^*)^{-1}X^{*\prime}Y^* = [b_0 \ b_1 \ldots b_k]' \qquad [6.4]$$

$$Y_p^* = X^*\beta^* \qquad [6.5]$$

$$E^* = Y^* - Y_p^* \qquad [6.6]$$

Y^* and X^* are matrices of quantitative (interval level) data values. They are functions of the original Y and X, respectively. The exact nature of the function f can differ from one variable to the next. It always depends upon the measurement characteristics of the variables; the function is used to provide the optimally scaled values for the observations. β^* is a $k \times 1$ vector of coefficients from the regression of Y^* on X^*. Y_p^* is a vector of predicted values for the optimally scaled dependent variable, and E^* is a residual, also calculated from the optimally scaled values.

All of the starred matrices of data values, as well as the coefficient vector, are estimated through an iterative procedure. On each iteration, there are two phases. Each phase minimizes the current value of $E^{*\prime}E^*$ (the sum of squared residual data values), subject to the appropriate constraints. First, there is the "model estimation phase" in which β^* is estimated, holding the current values of X^* and Y^* constant. As was obvious from equation 6.1 β^* is simply the OLS estimator calculated from the optimally scaled data. Because the Y^* and X^* are all measured at the interval level (regardless of the assumed measurement characteristics of the original Y and X), the interpretation of β^* is straightforward and requires no further discussion here.

Second, new values of Y^* and X^* are estimated, while holding the current values of β^* constant. This is the "optimal scaling phase" for the current iteration. In this phase, the previous data values (i.e., those used to calculate the current β^*) are transformed to maximize the fit of the model to the data (i.e., to minimize the value of $E^{*\prime}E^*$), while still conforming to the measurement characteristics that the analyst specified prior to the estimation. The optimal scaling is carried out separately for each variable. If a variable is measured at the nominal or ordinal levels, then Kruskal's monotone regression algorithm (1964) is used to find the optimal values. Briefly, this operates as follows: For each variable in the model, generate the set of model-based predicted values. For the dependent variable, this is simply Y_p^* from equation 6.2. For an independent variable, say, X_k, the values would be calculated as:

$$X_{kp}^* = [Y^* - (\Sigma X_j^* \beta_j^*)] / \beta_k \text{ (with } j \text{ not equal to } k) \qquad [6.7]$$

Now, take the means of the predicted values *within* the categories of the original variable. In other words, if there are M different categories of X_k (or Y), then there will be M different mean predicted values ($X_{kp}^*._c$ with $c = 1, 2, \ldots M$). At this point, it is necessary to distinguish between nominal and ordinal variables. If X_k is a set of nominal categories, then the $X_{kp}^*._c$ are themselves used as the optimally scaled values; they merely replace the previous values assigned to X_k^*. The $X_{kp}^*._c$ are the best-fitting values, because they are as close as possible to the model-based predicted values (X_{kp}^*) while still maintaining the nominal level conditions given back in equations 2.1 and 2.2.

If the variable is measured at the ordinal level, the ordering of the X_k^* values must be identical to the ordering of the original X_k categories. Whenever the $X_{kp}^*._c$ values are monotonically related to the X_k values, they are used, as is, for the X_k^*. But if monotonicity is violated in the predicted values (that is, $X_{kp}^*._1 > X_{kp}^*._2$ while $X_{k1} < X_{k2}$), the nonmonotonic $X_{kp}^*._c$ values are averaged until the resulting values are weakly monotonic with respect to the order of the original categories of X_k. These are used for the values of X_k^*. Once again, they are consistent with the necessary measurement level restrictions (equations 2.3 through 2.5), and they are the best least squares fit to the model-based predicted values.

Finally, if X_k is defined as an interval or ratio level variable, then X_k^* must be a specific function of the original values (e.g., linear). This can be handled by regressing the $X_{kp}^*._c$ on X_k, and using the predicted values from this regression as the new set of X_k^* values. By definition, this will be the best-fitting linear function between the original data values and the model-based predicted values.

Regardless of the assumptions about the measurement characteristics, the optimally scaled values replace the previous values in the appropriate data matrix (Y* or X*). The optimal scaling phase is completed when all variables have had their values updated in this manner.[30]

The procedure alternates between the two phases. Each one gives a least squares estimate of the appropriate parameters (model or measurement) while holding the other set of parameters constant at their current values. This is obviously the source of the term *alternating least squares, optimal scaling*. A model estimation phase, followed by an optimal scaling phase, constitutes an *iteration*. At the end of each iteration, the latest value of $E^{*'}E^*$ is calculated; after the first iteration, the current $E^{*'}E^*$ is compared to those calculated on the previous iteration(s). The procedure stops when the values of $E^{*'}E$ converge (i.e., they do not change from one iteration to the next), indicating that the best-fitting model has been found for the given set of observations.

The flow of the entire ALSOS regression algorithm is shown schematically in Figure 6.1. Given observation matrices Y and X, the analyst first specifies the measurement characteristics for all of the variables and chooses initial values for Y^* and X^*. The easiest way to do this is simply to set $Y^* = Y$ and $X^* = X$. The iteration process begins with the second step. This is the model estimation phase, where the β^* vector is calculated from the current Y^* and X^*. The R^2 is also calculated, and compared to the R^2 obtained from the previous iteration. If there is no significant improvement, the routine terminates. Otherwise, it proceeds to the next step. This is the optimal scaling phase, where the appropriate transformations are used to obtain new, better-fitting values for Y^* and X^*. Also, after each variable is scaled, it must be normalized in order to avoid trivial, degenerate solutions for the coefficients and the variable values. After all of the variables have been scaled and normalized, the procedure returns to step two for the next iteration.

The ALSOS algorithm continues until the R^2 values converge, showing that the model and measurement parameter estimates have not changed from one iteration to the next. The result is a set of "conditionally best-fitting" parameter estimates. This rather clumsy term refers to the fact that the final ALSOS results are always contingent upon the initial data values. But, given some initialization of the variables, the ALSOS routine does minimize the overall discrepancy between the statistical model and the measurement model for that particular set of observations.

The ALSOS strategy is not a panacea for the problems of analyzing qualitative data, and it certainly has limitations of its own. First, the ALSOS parameter estimates are conditional upon the initial values assigned to the variables. If a substantively equivalent, but numerically different set of variable values is used (e.g., a different assignment of numbers to the ordinal categories, or a different set of ordinal scores) then the parameter estimates could turn out to be quite different. Second, the quality of the optimally scaled data values depends upon the degree to which each variable can be predicted on the basis of the other variables in the model. But this is a matter of model specification, and the problem is equivalent to pointing out that the model should be well specified. A third limitation is that the ALSOS approach is entirely descriptive, rather than inferential, in nature. Although an ALSOS analysis enables a researcher to characterize the structure within a given set of observations,

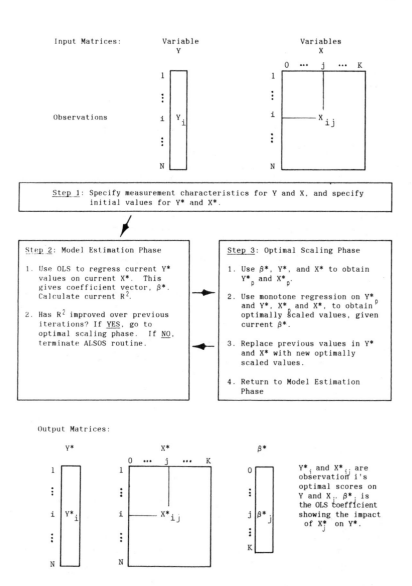

Figure 6.1. ALSOS Regression Algorithm

it provides no way to make statements about the population from which the observations are extracted.

The preceding disadvantages are offset by two advantages that the ALSOS approach possesses relative to other modeling techniques for qualitative variables. First, there is its sheer generality--the range of data analysis problems for which it can be used. In this discussion, we have only focused on a very simple situation: multiple regression with a set of discrete variables. It can easily be generalized to much more complex measurement characteristics: continuous variables, missing data, non-comparable partitions within a single variable, and so on. Perhaps more important, the ALSOS strategy can be used to estimate many other statistical models. In fact, because the model estimation is entirely separate from the optimal scaling, the ALSOS strategy can be used for virtually *any* kind of statistical analysis. As Young (1981) states, "If a procedure is known for obtaining a least squares description of numerical (interval or ratio measurement level) data, then an ALSOS algorithm can be constructed to obtain a least squares description of qualitative data (having a variety of measurement characteristics)" (p. 358).

The second advantage is that the ALSOS approach unifies the two types of models that are inherently involved in any empirical statistical analysis. Where traditional methods regard the data values as fixed quantities, the ALSOS strategy views them as an abstract model of the observations, the components of which can be manipulated according to certain specified rules. By taking this orientation, the ALSOS approach provides a useful way to examine hypotheses about *measurement,* apart from hypotheses about the structural coefficients in a statistical model. An ALSOS analysis can be repeated several times, using the same observations (i.e., initial data values) and statistical model, but altering the specification of measurement characteristics in the data. Of course, any differences in results would have to be attributable to the changes in the measurement characteristics. This, in turn, provides the researcher with some empirical basis for his or her measurement assumptions. In other words, if a variable that is assumed to be an ordinal level measure actually behaves like an interval level measure in an ALSOS analysis (i.e., the optimally scaled values are a linear function of the original data values), then it may as well be treated like an interval level variable until the evidence suggests otherwise. In this manner, the ALSOS approach encourages researchers to exploit the characteristics of their data aggressively in an effort to discern as clearly as possible the structure underlying their empirical observations.

7. CONCLUSIONS

There are three main conclusions to be drawn from the discussion in this monograph. First, data theory provides a comprehensive framework for understanding the information conveyed by empirical observations. This is important because it can direct researchers toward appropriate analytical procedures. It is hoped that such theory imposes a logical structure on the wide variety of scaling techniques available to the social science researcher. Data theory also suggests new ways for interpreting empirical observations. For example, it can be used to show how substantively different phenomena can sometimes be interpreted as the same kind of data, or how similar kinds of observations can be interpreted as different types of data, in order to generate different models of the empirical phenomena. In this way, data theory often helps to provide insights that would be overlooked otherwise.

Second, the distinction between "unidimensional" and "multidimensional" scaling models is essentially an artificial one. As emphasized here, dimensionality simply refers to the number of relevant differences among a set of objects. The four types of data are insensitive to this. In other words, dominance and proximity relations among point pairs can occur along a single number line, or in some space defined by several coordinate axes. The various scaling models are similar, in that the rules for moving from the data to the overall point configuration usually hold true regardless of the dimensionality of the space that contains the scaled points. Of course, the specific methods and algorithms may change from uni- to multidimensional applications. But these applications are really just the means toward an end. In every scaling analysis, the objective is to model the variability in the observations as accurately as possible. This may require several dimensions, or a single dimension may suffice. The choice between them is an empirical question.

Finally, it is important to emphasize again that measurement is always theory testing. The specific variable values used in any particular analysis are never immutable characteristics of the observations. Instead, they are simply the components of an abstract model. As such, they may provide a more or less accurate representation of some aspect of the empirical world. The emphasis in this monograph is that the parameters of any measurement model (i.e., the measurement level assumed, along with the specific data values assigned) should be subjected to empirical testing, rather than taken as a priori, unchangeable assumptions. This is particularly important in the social sciences, where critics often charge that the analytic techniques far exceed the capacities of the data. By explicitly testing our measurement characteristics, we should be able to formulate responses to these critics. And in so doing, researchers will be able to exploit their data to the greatest possible extent.

NOTES

1. Formal measurement theory, a branch of applied mathematics, is concerned with the conditions that must exist in order to apply numbers to objects. The major work in this field is Krantz, Luce, Suppes, and Tversky (1972). For a brief, accessible introduction, see Coombs, Dawes, and Tversky (1970), Chapter 2.

2. Some analysts contend that not all measurement theories are falsifiable. Dawes (1972) distinguishes between *representational* measurement and *index* measurement. The former involves a two-way correspondence between empirical observations and real numbers: The behavior of the empirical objects constrains the numerical assignments, and the assigned numbers lead to predictions about the behavior of the objects. Index measures only imply a one-way correspondence: The empirical objects are assigned numbers, but there is no way to "work backwards" from the numbers to the behavior of the objects. Accordingly, index measures cannot be tested directly. A single-item rating scale is the clearest example of an index measure. The use of index measures is justified on pragmatic grounds: They are helpful in understanding *other* interesting phenomena (e.g., a person's rating of a presidential candidate helps the analyst predict that individual's future voting behavior).

3. Along with measurement *levels,* Young (1987) identifies two other characteristics as follows. *Measurement process:* A set of numbers are either continuous (objects within a single category can be assigned different numbers, so long as assignments do not "overlap" between categories) or discrete (all objects in the same category are assigned a single number). *Measurement conditionality:* Determines which numbers can be directly compared to other numbers (e.g., missing data can be thought of as values that cannot be compared to the "real," nonmissing numeric values). For simplicity, we will not deal with measurement process and conditionality in this monograph.

4. With interval or ratio measurement, any specific function can be used to move from the objects to the numbers. Thus a polynomial such as $M(S_1) = a + (S_1)^b$ is perfectly acceptable as an interval level variable. In fact, this is the type of measurement model that is used for psychophysical magnitude scaling (Lodge, 1981). For most of the examples, we will continue to use the linear function, because it is the simplest form.

5. It is important to emphasize that *levels* of measurement are distinct and different from the *accuracy* of measurement. All measuring instruments have limits to their precision. This guarantees that the transformation from object to measure is never perfect. The imperfections that exist in the function transforming the substantive attribute into a set of numbers constitute measurement error. Obviously, this is a problem to be avoided (or its effects minimized)

wherever possible. However, the presence of measurement *error* does not, in any way, compromise the existence of a particular measurement *level*. The latter is based on the transformation from object set S to number set M. Measurement errors "fuzz" this process, but they do not eliminate it.

6. Even though each observation involves a distinct *pair* of points, a single point is usually involved in many such pairs. Thus, in the two observations "the apple is red" and "the berry is red," the "red" point is common to both observations. Of course, "apple" and "berry" would correspond to different points, thereby making the pairs different. Also, note that a single empirical observation can sometimes be broken down into several point pairs. Thus "the apple is red, and not yellow" involves two separate point pairs (apple-red, and apple-yellow).

7. In an earlier and extremely influential version of his data theory, Coombs (1964) suggested that observations varied according to three dichotomous distinctions: (1) They could involve a *pair* of points, or a pair of point pairs, called a *dyad;* (2) they could involve entities drawn from one or two sets; and (3) the relations between entities could be based upon dominance or proximity. Obviously, the latter two distinctions are precisely those in the data theory used here. The first distinction (pair versus dyad) is much less important to modern scaling strategies, primarily as a result of methodological developments that occurred after the publication of *A Theory of Data* (for a discussion about this, see Young, 1987). Therefore, the two dichotomous distinctions used here should be entirely sufficient for representing the different kinds of data commonly encountered in empirical analyses.

8. Some analysts (e.g., Coombs, 1964) discuss a property of scaling procedures called *vulnerability.* This refers to a procedure's tolerance for scaling errors — that is, the amount of error that can be present and still allow the procedure to generate a scaling solution. Procedures that are highly vulnerable (such as Coombs's original unidimensional unfolding technique) are more useful as scaling criteria, because they immediately indicate that a particular dimensional model cannot work with the data. Procedures that are less vulnerable (e.g., Likert scales) are more useful as scaling techniques because they permit the construction of a scale, even though substantial amounts of error may be present. The vulnerability property is less important than it was in the past, given that there are fewer pencil-and-paper scaling algorithms still in frequent use. Instead, computerized scaling routines usually give the best-fitting scaling solution, regardless of the amount of error that may be present.

9. The equal-appearing interval scale usually takes the *median* entry in each row of the data matrix, rather than the sum or a weighted sum, like the mean. Nevertheless, the median is still used as a measure of the row object's central tendency across the column objects; that is, it "cancels out" the fluctuations that occur within each row. Therefore it is the same model from a data theory perspective.

10. Analysts have been very hesitant to apply the polychotomous cumulative scaling model in actual research situations. Guttman (1947) seemed to suggest that polychotomous scales would never achieve high enough levels of reproducibility. And Coombs points out that there are problems involved in interpreting the goodness of fit measures for a polychotomous Guttman scale. These problems arise because the cutting points are perfectly scalable *within* categories of the original, polychotomous items. Most of these problems seem to have been overcome by combining the polychotomous cumulative model with the probabilistic formulation provided by Mokken (1970). Molenaar (1982) provides a detailed discussion of this approach. There is software available for analyzing the polychotomous, probabilistic cumulative scaling model. The program is called MSP (Mokken Scales for Polychotomies), and it is available from IEC-ProGamma, Kraneweg 8, 9718 JP, Groningen, The Netherlands.

11. There is, in fact, a multidimensional generalization of the Guttman Scalogram procedure (Zvulun, 1978). However, the methods are fairly cumbersome, and they seldom seem to be used in actual, substantive research contexts.

12. Communalities must be specified a priori in most factor analyses before proceeding.

13. There is actually an additional matrix generated in a factor analysis solution. This is a K by K diagonal matrix, in which the nonzero entries show each variable's dependency on a factor that is unique to itself. In other words, the unique factors each affect only a single variable; they are uncorrelated with all other observed variables and unobserved factors. When the values in this matrix are squared, they give the part of each observed variable's variance that is *not* accounted for by the M latent, common factors.

14. If the factors are assumed to be correlated with each other, then the factor analysis produces a second matrix: the factor structure matrix gives the correlations between the factors and the empirical variables. In the orthogonal factor solution, the factor pattern matrix and the factor structure matrix are identical.

15. The vector geometry of linear models is covered in most intermediate to advanced econometrics tests, such as Wonnacott and Wonnacott (1979).

16. This figure corresponds to the plot of the factor pattern that can be generated from the factor analysis routines contained in statistical software packages such as SPSS-X and SAS.

17. The scalar product is essentially the vector version of matrix multiplication. The scalar product of two vectors, say, X and Y, is defined as the sum of the products of their corresponding elements. Thus $XY = \Sigma\ X_iY_i$. Geometrically, the scalar product between two vectors is the length of the first vector times the length of the second vector times the cosine of the angle between the two vectors.

18. However, stimulus comparison data have a long history in experimental applications. Coombs (1964) states that stimulus comparison data "is the only kind that rivals single stimulus data in popularity" (p. 345). In fact, much of the impetus for the development of scaling methods in general can be traced back to the early work by L. L. Thurstone, much of which concentrated on stimulus comparison data.

19. Similarity values can always be reversed by multiplying each value by -1. This preserves all of the information in ordinal, interval, and ratio level similarities data. For ordinal and interval similarities, the values can be subtracted from some arbitrary constant to form dissimilarities.

20. This model can be fitted to a matrix of asymmetric dissimilarities by specifying the appropriate model option in the ALSCAL routine (which is available in both SPSS-X and in SAS).

21. The GEMSCAL model can be fitted by specifying the appropriate model option in ALSCAL.

22. For example, it is possible to conduct both nonmetric factor analyses (e.g., Shepard and Kruskal, 1974) and to factor analyze a three-way data matrix (e.g., Tucker, 1964).

23. There is a special situation in which correlations are monotonically related to interpoint distances: This occurs when all of the points are located at the same distance from the origin (Rabinowitz, 1975). Coxon (1982) points out that this is equivalent to standardizing the coordinate axes. But this does not exhaust the problems associated with the correlation coefficient. Rabinowitz (1973) shows that the correlation will depend upon the distribution of points in the space, as well as the distances between the points. For a similar argument, see Jones (1974).

24. Profile distances can be obtained by using the PROXIMITIES subprogram in SPSS-X, and PROC PROX in SAS.

25. The unfolding model can be generalized to handle a variety of more complicated situations, including three-way data matrices, and weights for subjects and/or stimuli. Carroll (1972) and Young (1987) both cover many varieties of the unfolding model. One interesting variation is sometimes called the "vector model for preferences." In this model, each subject is shown as a vector oriented within a multidimensional space. The stimuli are points in the space, which are projected onto each subject's vector. The higher the point projection (i.e., the greater the distance from the origin, along the subject's vector), the greater the preference of that subject for that stimulus. Carroll (1972) points out that this is still equivalent to the more common ideal points model; it is just that the ideal point for each subject is now located at an infinitely large distance from the origin of the joint space.

26. Carroll (1972) also shows that once the stimulus point configuration is known, the subjects' ideal points can be estimated using regression analysis — no special scaling software is required.

27. One variant of the proximity model occurs when all subjects choose the same number of stimuli. In this case, the solid bands of 1s in each row of the permuted data matrix would have uniform width. Accordingly, this is called "parallelogram scaling." An important advantage of this model over the more general proximity model is that it generates an unambiguous partial ordering of the ideal points— essentially, a categorical, ordinal variable measuring subjects' locations along the latent dimension (Coombs, 1964).

28. van Schuur (1984) also makes a general argument that dichotomous preference data are often more valid than the fully rank-ordered preferences usually used for unfolding analyses. The MUDFOLD program is available from IEC-ProGAMMA.

29. A closely related philosophy of data analysis, along with an extensive discussion of approaches and models, is provided in Gifi (1981).

30. Young (1981) lists the sources for software capable of performing ALSOS analyses, using a wide variety of statistical models. In addition, SAS includes a function called OPSCAL, which will provide an optimally scaled version of the values in a data vector. With the OPSCAL function, it is extremely easy to use PROC IML in SAS in order to program one's own ALSOS algorithms.

REFERENCES

ABBOTT, E. A. (1983) *Flatland (rev. 5 ed.)*. New York: Harper & Row.

ANDRICH, D. (1988) *Rasch Models for Measurement.* Newbury Park, CA: Sage.

ARABIE, P., CARROLL, J. D., and DeSARBO, W. S. (1987) *Three-Way Scaling and Clustering.* Newbury Park, CA: Sage.

BAKER, B. O., HARDYCK, C. D., PETRINOVICH, L. F. (1966) "Weak measurement versus strong statistics: An empirical critique of S. S. Stevens' proscriptions on statistics." *Educational and Psychological Measurement* 26: 291-309.

BLALOCK, H. M. (1982) *Conceptualization and Measurement in the Social Sciences.* Beverly Hills, CA: Sage.

CARROLL, J. D. (1972) "Individual differences and multidimensional scaling," in R. N. Shepard, A. K. Romney, and S. B. Nerlove (eds.) *Multidimensional Scaling. Volume I, Theory.* New York: Seminar.

CARROLL, J. D., and ARABIE, P. (1980) "Multidimensional scaling." *Annual Review of Psychology* 31: 607-649.

CARROLL, J. D., and CHANG, J. J. (1970) "Analysis of individual differences in multidimensional scaling via an N-way Generalization of 'Eckart-Young' decomposition." *Psychometrika* 35: 238-319.

COOMBS, C. H. (1953) "Theory and methods of social measurement," in L. Festinger and D. Katz (eds.) *Research Methods in the Behavioral Sciences.* New York: Dryden Press.

COOMBS, C. H. (1964) *A Theory of Data.* Ann Arbor, MI: Mathesis.

COOMBS, C. H., DAWES, R. M., and TVERSKY, A. (1970) *Mathematical Psychology: An Elementary Introduction.* Ann Arbor, MI: Mathesis.

COOMBS, C. H. RAIFFA, H., and THRALL, R. M. (1954) "Some views on mathematical models and measurement theory." *Psychological Review* 61: 132-144.

COOMBS, C. H., and SMITH, J. E. H. (1973) "On the detection of structure in attitudes and developmental processes." *Psychological Review* 80: 337-351.

COXON, A. P. M. (1982) *The User's Guide to Multidimensional Scaling.* Exeter, NH: Heinemann Educational Books.

DAVISON, M. L. (1983) *Multidimensional Scaling.* New York: John Wiley.

DAWES, R. M. (1972) *Fundamentals of Attitude Measurement.* New York: John Wiley.

DeSARBO, W. S., and CARROLL, J. D. (1985) "Three-way metric unfolding via alternating least squares." *Psychometrika* 50: 275-300.

EDWARDS, A. L. (1957) *Techniques of Attitude Scale Construction.* New York: Appleton-Century-Crofts.

GAITO, J. (1980) "Measurement scales and statistics: Resurgence of an old misconception." *Psychological Bulletin* 87: 564-567.

GIFI, A. (1981) *Nonlinear Multivariate Analysis.* Leiden, The Netherlands: University of Leiden.

GUTTMAN, L. (1945) "Questions and answers about scale analysis." Research Branch, Information and Education Division, Army Service Forces, Report D-2.

GUTTMAN, L. (1947) "On Festinger's evaluation of scale analysis." *Psychological Bulletin* 44: 451-465.

JONES, B. D. (1974) "Some considerations in the use of nonmetric multidimensional scaling." *Political Methodology* 1: 1-30.

KAPLAN, A. (1964) *The Conduct of Inquiry.* Scranton, PA: Chandler.

KIM, J. O., and MUELLER, C. W. (1978a) *Introduction to Factor Analysis.* Beverly Hills, CA: Sage.

KIM, J. O., and MUELLER, C. W. (1978b) *Factor Analysis.* Beverly Hills, CA: Sage.

KRANTZ, D. H., LUCE, R. D., SUPPES, P., and TVERSKY, A. (1972) *Foundations of Measurement.* New York: Academic Press.

KRUSKAL, J. B. (1964) "Multidimensional scaling by optimizing goodness of fit to a nonmetric hypothesis." *Psychometrika* 29: 1-28, 115-129.

KRUSKAL, J. B., and WISH, M. (1978) *Multidimensional Scaling.* Beverly Hills, CA: Sage.

LODGE, M. (1981) *Magnitude Scaling.* Beverly Hills, CA: Sage.

LONG, J. S. (1983) *Confirmatory Factor Analysis.* Beverly Hills, CA: Sage.

LORD, F. M. (1953) "On the statistical treatment of football numbers." *American Psychologist* 8: 750-751.

McCUTCHEON, A. L. (1987) *Latent Class Analysis.* Newbury Park, CA: Sage.

McIVER, J. P. and CARMINES, E. G. (1981) *Unidimensional Scaling. Beverly Hills, CA: Sage.*

MICHELL, J. (1986) "Measurement scales and statistics: A clash of paradigms." *Psychological Bulletin* 100: 398-407.

MOKKEN, R. J. (1970) *A Theory and Procedure of Scale Analysis.* The Hague: Mouton.

MOKKEN, R. J., and LEWIS, C. (1982) "A nonparametric approach to the analysis of dichotomous response items." *Applied Psychological Measurement* 4: 417-430.

MOLENAAR, I. W. (1982) "Mokken scaling revisited." *Kwantitatieve Methoden* 3: 145-164.

NIEMOLLER, K., and VAN SCHUUR, W. (1983) "Stochastic models for unidimensional scaling," in D. McKay, N. Schofield, and P. Whitely (eds.) *Data Analysis and the Social Sciences.* London: Pinter.

RABINOWITZ, G. B. (1973) *Spatial Models of Electoral Choice.* Chapel Hill, NC: Institute for Research in Social Science.

RABINOWITZ, G. B. (1975) "An introduction to nonmetric multidimensional scaling." *American Journal of Political Science* 19: 343-390.

RABINOWITZ, G. B. (1976) "A procedure for ordering object pairs consistent with the multidimensional unfolding model." *Psychometrika* 41: 349-373.

RODGERS, J. L., and YOUNG, F. W. (1981) "Successive unfolding of family preferences." *Applied Psychological Measurement* 5: 51-62.

ROSKAM, E. E. (1977) "The nature of data: Interpretation and representation — an introduction to the theory of data," in J. C. Lingoes, E. E. Roskam, and I. Borg (eds.) *Geometric Representations of Relational Data." Ann Arbor, MI: Mathesis.*

SCHIFFMAN, S. S., REYNOLDS, M. L., and YOUNG, F. W. (1981) *Introduction to Multidimensional Scaling.* New York: Academic Press.

SHEPARD, R. N. (1972) "A taxonomy of principal types of data and of multidimensional methods for their analysis," in R. N. Shepard, A. K. Romney, and S. B. Nerlove (Eds.) *Multidimensional Scaling. Volume I, Theory.* New York: Seminar.

SHEPARD, R. N., and KRUSKAL, J. B. (1974) "A nonmetric variety of linear factor analysis." *Psychometrika* 39: 123-147.

STEVENS, S. S. (1946) "On the theory of scales of measurement." *Science* 103: 677-680.

STEVENS, S. S. (1951) "Mathematics, measurement and psychophysics," in S. S. Stevens (ed.) *Handbook of Experimental Psychology.* New York: John Wiley.

STEVENS, S. S. (1957) "On the psychophysical law." *Psychological Review* 64: 153-181.

STEIGER, J. H., and SCHONEMANN, P. H. (1978) "A history of factor indeterminacy," in S. Shye (ed.) *Theory Construction and Data Analysis in the Behavioral Sciences.* San Francisco: Jossey-Bass.

THOMPSON, P. A. (1988) "A review of unfolding models and methods." Working Paper 88-31. Columbus: College of Business, Ohio State University.

TORGERSON, W. S. (1958) *Theory and Methods of Scaling.* New York: John Wiley.

TOWNSEND, J. T., and ASHBY, F. G. (1984) "Measurement scales and statistics: The misconception misconceived." *Psychological Bulletin* 96: 394-401.

TUCKER, L. R. (1964) "The extension of factor analysis to three-dimensional matrices," in N. Frederikson and H. Gulliksen (eds.) *Contributions to Mathematical Psychology.* New York: Holt, Rinehart & Winston.

VAN SCHUUR, W. H. (1984) *Structure in Political Beliefs.* Amsterdam: CT Press.

VAN SCHUUR, W. H. (1988) "Stochastic unfolding," in W. E. Saris and I. N. Gallhofer (eds.) *Sociometric Research. Volume I: Data Collection and Scaling.* London: Macmillan.

88

WEISBERG, H. F. (1972) "Scaling models for legislative roll-call analysis." *American Political Science Review* 66: 1306-1315.

WEISBERG, H. F. (1974) "Dimensionland: An excursion into spaces." *American Journal of Political Science* 18: 743-776.

WEISBERG, H. F. (1991) *Variance.* Newbury Park, CA: Sage.

WONNACOTT, R. J., and WONNACOTT. T. H. (1979) *Econometrics (2 ed.).* New York: John Wiley.

YOUNG, F. W. (1981) "Quantitative analysis of qualitative data." *Psychometrika* 46: 357-388.

YOUNG, F. W. (1987) "Theory," in F. W. Young and R. M. Hamer (eds.) *Multidimensional Scaling.* Hillsdale, NJ: Lawrence Erlbaum.

YOUNG, F. W., DE LEEUW, J., and TAKANE, Y. (1976) "Regression with quantitative and qualitative variables: An alternating least squares method with optimal scaling features." *Psychometrika* 41: 505-529.

ZVULUN, E. (1978) "Multidimensional scalogram analysis: The method and its application," in S. Shye (ed.) *Theory Construction and Data Analysis in the Behavioral Sciences.* San Francisco: Jossey-Bass.

ABOUT THE AUTHOR

WILLIAM G. JACOBY is an Assistant Professor of Government and International Studies at the University of South Carolina. He received his B.A. from the University of Delaware, and his M.A. and Ph.D. in Political Science from the University of North Carolina at Chapel Hill. Along with scaling methods and dimensional analysis, his major areas of interest are public opinion and political behavior. Dr. Jacoby has published articles in such journals as the *American Journal of Political Science* and the *Journal of Politics.* He is currently working on a study of ideological thinking in the American electorate.